the

INSTITUTES
of
BIBLICAL
LAW

The Intent of the Law

Volume Three

the

INSTITUTES
of

BIBLICAL

LAW

The Intent of the Law

Rousas John Rushdoony

ROSS HOUSE BOOKS
VALLECITO, CALIFORNIA
95251

Library of Congress Catalog Card Number: 99-074419
ISBN:1-879998-13-0

Printed in the United States of America

This printing was made possible by

the labors of

Bob and Mary Helen

of

Bob Green Expert Tree Service

Vallecito, California

1970-1997

To my children:
Rebecca Jean Rouse,
Joanna May Manesajian,
Sharon Rose North,
Martha Lee Coie,
and Mark Rousas Rushdoony;

and to my grandchildren:
Sarah Rouse Nunes, Jill Rouse, Levi Rouse, Emily Rouse;
Rachel Manesajian, Daniel Manesajian;
Darcy North, Scott North, Lori North, Caleb North;
Christine Coie Aardema, Jennifer Coie, Mary Coie, Glenn Coie;
Isaac Rushdoony, April Rushdoony, Marie Rushdoony, Ross Rushdoony;
and to my great grand-daughter, Brittney Nunes,
and to the great-grandchild to be born shortly to Christine and Dean Aardema.

May God's grace and blessings surround you
and make you ever faithful to Him.

Other books by
Rousas John Rushdoony

The Institutes of Biblical Law, Vol. I
The Institutes of Biblical Law, Vol. II, Law & Society
Systematic Theology
Sovereignty
The Cure of Souls
Foundations of Social Order
Politics of Guilt and Pity
Christianity and the State
Salvation and Godly Rule
The Messianic Character of American Education
Roots of Reconstruction
The One and the Many
Revolt Against Maturity
By What Standard?
Law & Liberty

For a complete listing of available books
by Rousas John Rushdoony and other
Christian reconstructionists, contact:

ROSS HOUSE BOOKS
PO Box 158
Vallecito, CA 95251

Table of Contents

Table of Contents

Preface

With this volume, I conclude my studies in Biblical law, knowing that more needs to be said, but that, at age 81, I cannot say it all. At one time, all Christendom recognized God's law as the governing word for men and nations. We have seen, in this century especially, a major revolt against God's enscriptured law. The consequences are not good for men or nations. It is an illusion to believe that men can live without law. In a fallen world, with men in revolt against God, God's law is the only effective and valid check against evil, the only true way of justice, and the necessary condition of life.

Writing the *Institutes of Biblical Law*, volumes I and II, certainly brought on me savage hostilities, both from the world at large, but also from the church. It is very important that I add that it has brought even greater blessings.

I have tried, over the years, to do four interconnected things. *First*, to honor and to further the presuppositionalist philosophy of religion of Dr. Cornelius Van Til. *Second*, to further a return to a Christian education as against the prevailing statist and humanist philosophies and practices on all levels of education. *Third*, I have sought to recall men to the law-word of God. So much of the Bible, including the prophets and the historical books, is given to this that it seems strange that one could see dispensing with most of the Bible as valid! But there is a *fourth* one, namely, to set forth, systematically and Biblically, theology, the Biblical perspective for all of life and thought. We cannot limit Christian theology to church life without denying it.

As I have grown older, I have grown steadily more appreciative of the love, training, and heritage given to me by my father and mother. There is a beautiful phrase in the Bible that I think often of, namely, that someone "died and was gathered unto his people," or fathers (Gen. 25:8, 17; 35:29; 49:29, 33). This happy event lies ahead of me. I think too of the many friends and supporters, some now dead, many still living, and the privileges of eternity in so blessed a company. I thank God that by His sovereign grace I was born rich and will die even richer.

Rousas John Rushdoony
Chalcedon, October 18, 1997

Note: The appendix, "The Private and the Public Domain," I wrote for the Notre Dame Law Review, *vol. 71, no. 1, 1996. That issue was in honor of the late Edward J. Murphy, at one time dean and a professor of the University of Notre Dame School of Law. Dr. Murphy was a faithful friend and truly a theonomist. It was a privilege to be his friend.*

i

Chapter One
The Necessity for Biblical Law

According to the rabbinic reckoning, the Torah has 613 laws. In terms of Christian tallies, the number is somewhat less because the ancient rabbinic count sometimes divides a single statement into more than one law. Whichever approach to counting laws is used, a very significant fact emerges.

God's purpose is that all of society, and all men and nations, be governed by His law. Now the laws of any particular state or nation in our present world order cannot be comprehended in 613 large law books, let alone 613 laws. God obviously does not purpose that a nation's laws cover all things, nor govern all things.

Men bridle at God's law because it legislates against sin. They prefer an order that permits sin and forbids freedom. They see God's law as tyranny because it is a control on sin whereas they prefer controls on freedom and a license to sin. We have seen what Judge Harold J. Rothwax has called an "affection for formalism...that stabs at the heart of our most precious moral values."[1]

The words *justice* and *righteousness* are in the Bible one and the same. In practice today, there is little relationship between them. Such a separation spells the death of a culture.

There is another important aspect to God's law, to Biblical law. It may seem to a modern lawyer or judge that 613 laws are too few. The truth is even more radical. As we shall see, of the 613 laws, many are not enforceable by man, but only by God. This means that the jurisdictions of church and state are very limited. We have here a godly libertarianism which severely limits the powers of all human agencies. Biblical law seems oppressive only to those who want freedom to sin. God's laws have as their purpose *our good*. In Deuteronomy 10:13, God orders us through Moses

> To keep the commandments of the LORD, and his statutes, which I command thee this day for thy good.

It does not say much for the character of those churchmen who see salvation as freedom from keeping the law. Through Jesus Christ, we are freed from the *condemnation* of the law, its death penalty, into power to live within the law, now written on the tables of our hearts (Ezek. 36:25-28; Jer. 31:33-34).

God delivered His law through Moses *to the people* of Israel, primarily, not to their institutions except secondarily. It is persons who must keep the law. Since it is *for our good*, God's law is for us "the perfect law of liberty" (Jam. 1:25). If we neglect that law, we neglect our liberty and fall into bondage to state and church.

---

[1] Harold J. Rothwax, *Guilty, The Collapse of Criminal Justice* (New York, N.Y.: Random House, 1996), p. 99.

Guilty men are not free men. In our time, placing people under a "guilt trip"
has become commonplace and a form of enslavement. We *are* guilty if we violate
God's law, but we cannot be bound in conscience by man's law. It is expedient
that we often obey man-made laws because we are not called to change the world
by lawlessness and revolution but through Jesus Christ. Regeneration, not
revolution, must be our way.

We must recognize that as Christians for us the *first* and most basic
government is the self-government of the Christian man. Without this, we have
nations of slaves. Then, *second,* the basic governmental institution is the family,
man's first sphere of government, his first church and school, his first area of
economic knowledge, and so on and on. *Third*, the church is a government;
fourth, so too is the school. *Fifth*, our vocation governs us, and, *sixth*, so too does
the society we live in, its private and public associations, and so on. *Seventh, civil*
government, the state, one government among many, also governs us.

God's law provides us with His law for every sphere. It alone can equip us to
resist the encroachment of alien powers. It alone empowers the individual
person and the family to govern properly.

We cannot expect our present-day church and state to be favorable to God's
law, because it denies to them powers they claim and use.

There is now a great governmental change under way. With the Christian
school and home-school movements under way, we see more and more families
taking back one sphere of government from the state. This represents a major
movement against the forces of the Enlightenment and statism.

There is also a growing recognition that the source of law is the god of a
people or country, and the modern state is the god of the modern age.
Sovereignty belongs to God, and He is therefore the only valid source of law.
The first edition of the *Encyclopaedia Britannica* (1771, vol. 2, p. 862) began its
study of law by defining it as "The command of the sovereign power, containing
a common rule of life for the subjects." Whose law we acknowledge as our true
law is our god and sovereign. Too many churchmen, by denying the validity of
God's law, acknowledge thereby that they worship a false god, and they do this
shamelessly. They say in effect with Pharaoh, "Who is the LORD, that I should
obey his voice?" (Ex. 5:2). To *obey God* means to obey His law, His
commandments.

W. A. Whitehouse said of the words *obey* and *obedience* that in the Hebrew it is
to hear. It simply tells us that to hear God is to obey Him. This is also true of the
Greek word translated as *obey*. The contrast to *hear* and *obey* is *revolt* or *disobedience*.
The word is used covenantally. The response to God's covenant of grace and
law is properly to hear and obey.[2]

[2.] W.A. Whitehouse, "Obey, Obedience," Alan Richardson, editor, *A Theological Word Book of the Bible* (New York, N.Y.: Macmillan (1950) 1960), p. 160.

Since the law is for our good, it is a personal communication from God to Israel, to a fallen world, and to the church and the nations. There is nothing personal about an act of Congress, Parliament, or any like body. Rather, it is very strictly impersonal and technical; it lends itself to nit-picking and misuse. God's law is the personal word for our good, from the totally personal God. We are sometimes told, in a revealing phrase, that a crime reported to an agency of state sets *the machinery* of the law to work. This expresses the cold, impersonal operation of man's, or the state's, law. Not so with God. The Bible speaks of *the wrath of God*; nothing could be less impersonal! Sin is a totally personal offense against a totally personal God. Many people simply misunderstand the Bible and try to give less personal meanings to many expressions, and this warps their meaning. For example, God in Numbers 12:14 rejects Moses' attempt to depersonalize Miriam's offense and punishment by stressing the personal offensiveness of Miriam and her sin, saying,

> If her father had but spit in her face, should she not be ashamed seven days? let her be shut out from the camp seven days, and after that let her be received in again.

To depersonalize God is also to depersonalize ourselves.

If, as Scripture makes clear, we are to live by what at most can be called 613 laws, then we cannot have a power-state nor a power-church, because their sphere of relevance is limited to a very few of those 613 laws. It means also that those laws of the 613 which are not reserved by God to His own enforcement, or are given to state and church, are placed in the hands of individuals and families. The Christian must thus be a grace-man and a law-man: he must manifest both and become their walking manifestation.

Grace in the Old Testament is "kindness and graciousness in general — that is, where there is no particular tie or relationship between the persons concerned. Further, it is shown by a superior to an inferior, and there is no obligation on the part of the superior to show this kindness." This meaning is strongly developed in the New Testament.[3]

Grace and *law* are covenantal. God's covenant is a covenant of grace because for Him to enter into a covenant or treaty with man is an act of grace from the superior to the inferior. At the same time, a covenant is a treaty of law whereby in this case the greater tells the lesser how to live under His care and protection. To reject God's law is to reject His grace whereby He gives us His law *for our good*. To reject or to break God's covenant is to invite and be under His judgment, and this we have done.

Judgment is both covenantal and personal. God is a Person; His law is personal, and so too is His judgment. Since the Enlightenment, men have steadily depersonalized their lives, the world, and the universe. Sir Isaac

---

[3.] N.H. Smith, "Grace," in Alan Richardson, *ibid.*, p. 100f.

Newton's physics was hailed as a triumph, and Newton as an incomparably great man, because he depersonalized the universe. For many deists, Newton also in effect depersonalized whatever god might exist. He was at best the Great Mechanic.

Since then, we have depersonalized all of life, including the state. This was easier to do once kings were eliminated and replaced by the mechanics of statecraft in the form of a *method* of government, not in itself wrong but deadly in the context of cultural depersonalization.

We can *know* persons, but can we know 613 or 60,013 law books? We can know God, who changes not (Mal. 3:6), but can we know the state, whose laws or character constantly change?

And what is law, if it constantly changes at the will of men? If an act of Congress can redefine good and evil, or if courts can legalize abortion, homosexuality, and euthanasia, why not rape and murder? If the state defines morality, what happens to good and evil, or to truth?

We are in the latter stages of the growing decay and collapse of statist law. It is time to reconsider God's law. Our freedom depends on it.

Chapter Two
The Laws of Sacrifice

Sacrificial offerings:

1. Peace offering: Leviticus 7:11-18, 28-34; 3:1-17; 17:1-9; 19:5-8; 22:21, 23; Exodus 29:19-26.

2. Sin offering: Leviticus 4:1-35; 5:1-13; 6:24-30; 8:14-15; 10:16-20. Scapegoat, for all Israel: Leviticus 16:20-22; Numbers 15:22-31; Exodus 29:11-14.

3. Guilt or trespass offering: Leviticus 5:14-19; 6:1-7; 7:1-7; 19:20-22; Numbers 5:5-8. For ignorance: Numbers 15:22-28.

4. Leprosy offering: Leviticus 13:47-59; 14:2-32, 43-57.

5. Burnt offering: Leviticus 1:3-17; 6:2-13; Exodus 18:12; 29:13-18; 1 Kings 3:4. Daily offering: Exodus 29:38-42; 30:7f.; Numbers 28:1-8.

6. Meat offering: Leviticus 2:1-13; 6:14-23; Numbers 15:1-10.

7. Jealousy offering: Numbers 5:11-31.

(In all the world, there are evidences of sacrifices, and in some areas they still survive. Men have attempted on their own to deal with the fact of sin, and have sought release from the burden of sin and guilt, on their own, but without success.)

One of the problems with any understanding of these laws governing sacrifices for sin is that they are usually described as *ceremonial* laws. Although so termed by excellent scholars, it is, I believe, a serious distortion of Scripture. The dictionary definition of "ceremonial" is "marked by, involved in, or belonging to ceremony: stressing careful attention to form and detail." This is true enough, but it does not do more than describe the care which must be given to every aspect of these laws, but their meaning lies elsewhere. These are laws of *sacrifice*; their purpose is to restore a broken relationship to God, or, to give thanks, to seek atonement, or some like urgent aspect of our duty to God. The word *ceremony* trivializes atonement, and all sacrifices generally.

A related problem is to see these laws as totally obsolete since Christ's atoning death. The sacrificial system is indeed ended since our Lord's vicarious sacrifice, but there is much to these laws of permanent validity. By God's providential government, these laws of sacrifice are a part of His infallible law-word. If their relevance was only until Christ's death, then why are they a part of His word? Or, why not skip over them in reading the Bible?

We do have some strange commentators who provide us with arcane meanings for everything connected with the tabernacle, its dimensions, colors, and materials. These are meanings which no devout readers can see on their own, and they lack a moral content.

5

But the laws of sacrifice have some very obvious meanings that cry out for recognition and observance. Consider, *first*, the difference between clean and unclean animals. Leviticus 11 defines for us at some length the difference between clean and unclean animals, a difference we must observe in our eating, for to eat unclean is called an "abomination." But not all clean animals are acceptable as sacrifices to God. Thus, trout and salmon are clean; fish, and deer are clean animals; but they are not acceptable at the altar of sacrifices. The clean animals which are acceptable to God for atonement, as a peace offering, or anything else are those in whose care and raising much of our labor, or later, some man's labor and our money, were involved.

This is an important fact, especially in our time when cheap, Arminian revivalism talks much about "free grace." It was not "free" for Jesus Christ: it cost Him the agony of crucifixion and a criminal's death. In return, our old man must die so that the new man might live. We do not coast into heaven (although we can into hell) because we are "saved to serve," and our Christian commitment can create vicious hostilities against us. If all this is no more than a ceremony, it is often a grim and painful one. St. Paul certainly did not coast into heaven. Isaac Watts (1724) rightly ridiculed, in his hymn, "Am I a Soldier of the Cross," the attitude of some:

> Must I be carried to the skies
> On flow'ry beds of ease,
> While others fought to win the prize,
> And sailed through bloody seas?

Then, *second*, what the laws of sacrifice tell us is that, as Hebrews 9:22 summarizes it, "And almost all things are by the law purged with blood; and without the shedding of blood is no remission" of sin. Sin is a very serious matter, a mortal concern. Moreover, the evaluation of sin does not rest on our will or our standards, but on God and His law-word. Men like to depreciate the validity of the law because they thereby depreciate the seriousness of their own sin and guilt. But we have here in God's law a strict description of the meaning and price of sin.

In Proverbs 30:20, we are told,

> Such is the way of an adulteress woman; she eateth, and wipeth her mouth, and saith, I have done no wickedness.

It is for her a trifle, as morally indifferent as eating food and wiping her mouth. More than a few men have excused their sin with the off-hand comment, "It was no big deal." The sacrificial system and the laws thereof tell us that God takes sin very seriously, even though we do not. Its price is the crucifixion of Jesus Christ.

Man's bent is to trivialize sin, especially his own. A confidence in one's integrity and good intentions leads us all to over-rate the sins of others while under-rating our own. The laws of sacrifice are not exciting reading, but they do remind us how serious sin is in God's sight. We take seriously, very seriously, many trifles while being uneasy, fretful, or unhappy that God takes seriously our own beloved sins.

Then, *third*, we are told, for example in Leviticus 22:20 and Deuteronomy 15:21, that a blemished sacrifice is not acceptable to God. The reverse of this view is prevalent today, especially in evangelical circles. All too many give to the church blemished gifts with the smug comment, "It's for the Lord," as though God is pleased to receive their left-overs. This kind of insult is routine in many circles. A companion law, in Leviticus 21:21, forbids any blemished or handicapped person from serving the Lord. The attitude of some is, How dare God discriminate? Implicit is the assumption, I, as a good humanist, refuse to discriminate. How dare God do so? Leviticus 21:16-20 lists some of the blemishes that bar a man, one of them being broken testicles. Do these good humanists insist their daughters marry such a man? *God sets the standards, not man.*

To give God our left-overs is to insult Him. The *requirement* that God receive our firstfruits means that He must come first, and He must receive our very best. After all, He is God, not we ourselves!

The sacrificial laws tell us that our relationship to God is a very serious matter, a matter of life and blood, and we dare not tamper with His requirements nor trivialize them.

We cannot make atonement for our sin because we are a blemished offering. Christ is our vicarious sacrifice. The sacrificial system tells us that we are blemished persons, radically blemished. As Christians by Christ's atoning sacrifice, our standing before God is by grace and in Christ. We have no independent avenue of approach to God, before or after our redemption. Without the sacrificial system, we are all dead men.

Fourth, basic to the sacrificial laws is restitution, or gratitude for the restored relationship. In Exodus 22, for example, we have laws of restitution for various offenses, ranging from twofold to fivefold restitution for our offenses against one another. The *required* restitution for man's rebellion against God is death; sin has death as its penalty (Rom. 5:12). Sin is, moreover, death, because it separates us from God. Our death then only accomplishes our death and reprobation. It requires the death of Jesus Christ, our sinless and unblemished substitute, to effect atonement for us. We are by His atonement made a new creation (2 Cor. 5:17). Having been made a new creation, we have a duty to bring our world, our every thought and activity, into captivity to Christ. In 2 Corinthians 10:5-6, we are told how radical a battle and victory is required of us. The perfection of God's creation (Gen. 1:31) must be restored in the developed glory under Christ.

The sacrificial system has as its purpose our restoration into God's grace and calling so that we might fulfil our creation mandate (Gen. 1:26-28). The fall was followed by the introduction of sacrifices, and Cain sought to avoid a sacrifice of atonement because he was unwilling to acknowledge that he was a sinner (Gen. 4:1-5).

Fifth, the words *offer, offering,* and related terms appear hundreds of times in connection with sacrifices. They speak of something due to God as Lord and Creator. Christ's offering of Himself for our atonement does not exhaust the requirement of sacrifice, and to think so is to reduce God to our servant when we are His servants and the sheep of His pasture (Ps. 23). Christ's atonement should increase our gratitude, and our gifts and offerings. We have lost a meaning of an offering, either of ourselves or of our substance, except for a minority of Christians.

An offering is a condition of peace with God. God, who needs nothing, requires an offering from us for our good. We are His servants, not He ours: He owes us nothing. David does *not* say, The LORD is my *servant*; I shall not want!

"Offerings…are the gifts of any kind of property to God."[1] It is a gift with no strings attached, a transfer of property and ownership. In the church too often the expectation has been that God should pour out His gifts upon us. God does indeed give men good gifts, but the expectation of such things as our due is an indication that the nature of the relationship of God and man has been reversed and is seriously defective.

Sixth, some sacrifices involve *the laying on of hands. Hands* represent skill and power. "A handy man" is one with a variety of talents. The laying on of hands can mean blessing someone, or transferring a function, or conferring a power. The hand is used in giving and receiving and therefore has a religious significance in certain acts. It could mean also the transfer of guilt. The worshipper, by the laying on of hands, identified himself with the sacrificial animal and saw the animal as his vicarious sin-bearer.

This means that a premise of sacrifice, was, *seventh, representation.* We are never members of a meaningless universe of brute factuality. All things are inter-related within the context of God's sovereign purpose. "The offering represents the offerer."[2] But the offerer cannot choose what will represent him, because the prerogative of designating approach rests with God. He alone can determine who can represent us and how. We cannot create our own means of representation and approach.

Eighth, sacrifices could include offerings made to make expiation for offenses against man. This could mean defrauding someone, or failure to return something left for safekeeping, for example. The sacrifice did not eliminate the requirement for restitution: it simply acknowledged that an offense against one's neighbor was and is a sin against God. It is God's law we violate when we sin against our neighbor, or any man.

---

[1] John Brown Paton, "Offerings," in *Imperial Standard Bible Encyclopedia*, vol. Five (Grand Rapids, Michigan: Zondervan, (1991), 1957), p. 54.
[2] *ibid.*, V., p. 55.

Ninth, not all the offerings were bloody sacrifices. Some were gift offerings of food, but all were *sacrifices* required of the believer although not bloody sacrifices on the altar. They were *gifts* to God's temple or house.

Tenth, in the New Testament, the communion service represents the culmination of the sacrificial system. In *Institutes of Biblical Law*, vol. II, in the discussion of the Sabbath and Community (pp. 1-109), I called attention to the fact that restoration into communion with God has as its requirement that we bring the human community together through Christ's atonement. His sacrifice of atonement requires our sacrificial efforts to make this world God's Kingdom. The purpose of Christ's work of atonement was to redeem us to be His people and to empower us to conquer all things in His Name. The purpose of the atonement was not to provide us with a problem-free and easy life but to make us "soldiers of the Cross," members in good standing in a life-long battle against sin and death.

The Cross is the end of the sacrificial system, but not of its meaning. If we isolate the Cross from the long history of sacrifices, we tend to stress only what Christ did for us, the rightly finished work. If we approach the atonement with the meaning of sacrifice in mind, we are enabled to recognize what Christ now expects of us.

What has been said here about sacrifices is simply to open up their meaning, and it does not by any means exhaust it.

Turning once again to their classification, as *ceremonial* laws, this term had its origins in pre-Reformation thinking. Because the medieval church had developed many rites and ceremonies on its own initiative, it used as its justification the *ceremonial* laws of the Old Testament. Too often the Protestant argument turned against the Old Testament rather than differentiating between Biblical law and church law. As a result, the Protestants allowed a false perspective to frame their argument.

Chapter Three
Tithes and Social Financing

1. Tithes on increase: Genesis 28:20-22; Leviticus 27:30-33; Numbers 18:21-26; Deuteronomy 14:22-29; 26:12-13.

2. Redemption of first-born sons: Exodus 13:1-2, 15; 22:29; 34:20; Numbers 3:11-13; 44-51; 8:16-18.

3. Redemption of first-born in flocks, herds: Exodus 13:11-13; 22:30; 34:14-20; Leviticus 27:26f.; Numbers 18:15-17; Deuteronomy 14:23-26; 15:19-22.

4. First fruits: Exodus 23:16-19; 34:26; Leviticus 19:23f.; 23:10f.; Numbers 15:17-21; Deuteronomy 18:1-11.

5. Monetary redemption: Deuteronomy 14:24-26.

(In *Tithing and Dominion* (1979), Edward A. Powell and I treated this general subject from the standpoint of tithing as God's appointed way for Christian dominion. What follows is not a repetition but is a development of the same thesis.)

In any society social financing must be provided unless that society, in some way imitating Sparta, wants to execute all unwanted peoples. This is a solution which various Marxist powers have adopted, and this answer is a brutal one and its methods radically vicious. It is a solution which may commend itself to many on the political left, but it is a mark of degeneracy rather than of wisdom.

There are those in the ministry who claim that tithing is now invalid because Christ has come. Where does Christ abolish the law? We are in Christ dead to the law as a handwriting of ordinances, and indictments against us calling for death; but we are alive to it as God's way of righteousness or justice, as our way of sanctification. Judging by the growing sexual misconduct in many church circles, including fornication, adultery, homosexuality, child abuse, and so on, it would seem that some are determined to reach heaven by illicit copulation.

In Matthew 23:23, and Luke 11:42, our Lord condemns the scribes and Pharisees for assuming that tithing will save them. He calls them "hypocrites," and says, "*These ought ye to have done*" but not to forgo obedience to "the weightier matters of the law, judgment, mercy, and faith." What will He say to those who forego tithing as well? To say that our Lord said this "before the Cross" is silly. Why was He so plain spoken about a fading concern? In Hebrews 7:5-9, tithing is clearly presented as important in Abraham's day and ours.

Social financing is a necessity in any and every society above the most backward level. If it is not provided by God's people, the state must step in and assume the responsibility, or face anarchy. Statist welfarism and social financing have been from antiquity a source of civil corruption, the destruction of the family, and a burden that can bring down the state.

11

God could have required that state and/or church make tithing mandatory and forcibly collect tithes. This would simply be a form of socialism, whether civil or ecclesiastical. It would also be a misuse of the tithe. A recent account of how much tax money reaches the needy reported that in one case appropriations equivalent to about $8,000 per person amounted to $300 when they reached their destination. Bureaucracy abounds in both church and state, as much as the available funds will provide.

God makes mandatory the *moral* obligation to care for widows, orphans, aliens, the needy, the sick, and so on and on, but He does not give either church or state the power to enforce the tithe. True enough, tithing has often enough been made mandatory, and it still is so in some European states not notable for their faith.

By not making tithing a matter of civil or ecclesiastical enforcement, God, in effect tells us that we shall have the kind of society we deserve. We are told thereby that if we do not obey Him, we shall suffer the consequences. There is a triple tithe required of us in the six years before the sabbath year: *first*, a tithe was given to the Levites, who gave a tithe of the tithe to the priests (Num. 18:25-28). This meant that one percent of ones' increase was so designated. The Levites, of course, provided for the care of the sanctuary, and its music. This is an annual tithe.

The *second* tithe, Deuteronomy 14:22-27, was for rejoicing before the Lord, together with the Levite. The family's rest and rejoicing are religiously required.

The *third* tithe, on the third and sixth years, was a poor tithe, to be shared with the local Levite, the stranger, the fatherless, the needy, the widow, etc. (Deut. 14:28-29).

Those who see these tithes as "too much" forget that they are paying far more in taxes for bad services to the state. In the 1990s, it is said that Americans are paying about 51 percent of their income in taxes to some agency of state, from the federal to the local level. And still we are abused as neglectful of some areas of human need! We are supporting the state and its agencies better than ourselves.

Socialism is a form of slavery. In some cultures, people have sold themselves into slavery in preference to freedom and its liabilities.[1] Slaves are often brutally treated, at other times indulgently so. At all times, they are no longer responsible for their support nor their future.

In our time, men talk much of freedom while working to create a slave state. God gives us the freedom to do this. The warning of God through Samuel (1 Sam. 8) has not been heeded over the centuries, nor is it heeded now.

Because the basic government is the self-government of the Christian man, what God tells us through His laws on tithing is that we must either establish

---

[1.] Alain Borer, *Rimbaud in Abyssinia* (New York, N.Y.: William Morrow, 1984), p. 221f.

freedom according to His word or have slavery as our destiny. Through tithing, we can provide social financing.

At one time, in the United States, tithe agencies met immigrants at the docks to offer help in finding homes and jobs, Christian schools for their children, classes for the women on a variety of subjects, and so on. The results were remarkable. We now seem to prefer socialism and slavery.

In the "medieval" era, the tithe was more or less enforced, and sometimes, because of its unpopularity, it was not even a tenth. Many reforms occurred as discontented peoples withheld their tithes and offerings from churchmen they regarded as wayward, non-Christian, or corrupt. New and reforming orders grew quickly as the people turned to them with their interest and support. Reformation was thus a continuing fact during the "medieval" era.

Two things helped choke off reform and made the explosion of the Reformation inevitable. *First*, tithes and gifts had to go to the parish church and other approved agencies alone. *Second*, attendance had to be to the local parish church.

The same two deadly factors now haunt the Protestant churches. Earlier in the twentieth century, some fundamentalist churches began to insist on the "storehouse" tithing, identifying the local church as the "storehouse" of Malachi 3:10. But the reference there is to an actual storehouse maintained by the Levites to receive such things as grains and livestock. The Levites would then sell and distribute the tithe as instructed. Such storehouses were once a part of the American scene, and some such buildings still survive.

God nowhere empowers the church or state with controls over the tithe. Abraham tithed to Melchizedek on his own volition (Heb. 7:4-6), and the man from Baal-shalisha gave his tithe to Elisha and the school of the prophets on his own (2 Kings 4:42-44). Elisha was definitely not a temple-approved recipient for tithes.

Tithing is a form of governing. Our gifts direct and govern churches and Christian agencies and causes. We as individuals are not infallible in our judgment, but, on the whole, we do as well and better than church and state. There are indeed causes which exploit gullible Christians, but, as in very recent years, when some deceptive causes and television evangelists were exposed, people largely stopped giving to them, and many failed. But when corruption in state agencies is exposed, the taxes continue. When a church's work in some sphere is exposed as bad, it does no good to withhold support for it because funds from other departments are directed into it. The administrator of tithing should be the tither; he is far from all-wise or perfect, but he is still more responsible. But, first, he must begin tithing. Otherwise the state must take over, and the man is then a loser of money and freedom.

The redemption of first-born sons (Ex. 13:1-2, 15) rests on the same premise as the tithe. All that we have and are belongs to God, and the requirement that the first-born sons must be set apart to be redeemed (Ex. 34:20; Num. 3:11-13, 44-51; 8:18) is to remind us that God has prior claim on everything that we are and have. We cannot live as our own governors and lords: we are God's property.

But man's original sin is to seek to be his own god and his own maker of law, his own determiner of good and evil (Gen. 3:5). The redemption of the first-born, typifying all, tells us that God claims the totality of our lives and possessions as His own. We have been created for His holy purposes, not our own, and any arrogant claim to independence on our part is a prescription for disaster.

The same applies to the first-born of flocks and herds. These must either be redeemed or given to God. At one time, some Christians recognized God's property rights here, although few do now.

All first-fruits, of grain or fruits, belong also to God and had to be taken to the sanctuary.

But the *last-fruits* are not ours either. In the laws of gleaning, the vines and trees could not be picked clean. The fruit on the top branches, the grain along the edges, and the stray bunches of grapes, had to be left for the gleaners (Lev. 19:9-10; Deut. 24:19-21). God thus governs every aspect of our lives and world, but He gives church and state limited jurisdiction over us. His enscriptured word speaks to us, not to church nor state.

The Lord God thus leaves the determination of our lives in our hands *under Him and His law-word*. Too often we sell our souls and freedom for a mess of ecclesiastical and/or civil pottage and slavery. Thus far, we have seen no laws entrusted to church or state for enforcement. God's purposes do not make either church nor state basic to His Kingdom. The family is often in God's law, and the family is God's most important institution. He takes His own designation, *Father*, from the family.

It is individuals and families who suffer most from tyranny, and it is they who must be zealous for freedom by providing social financing which will meet the needs God requires us to meet without creating a power state. God's appointed means of social financing are tithes and offerings or gifts. A tithe is God's tax; only when we go beyond the tithe have we given a gift to God and His work. Too many want neither to pay their tax nor to make a gift. All such people are really opting for tyranny and slavery.

Many who claim to be champions of freedom are really promoters of slavery. They believe that appeals to certain laws will provide them with the tools whereby liberty will be restored. They are opting for revolution, not regeneration, for slavery, not for freedom. The Christian premise of freedom is man's regeneration in Christ, "If the Son therefore shall make you free, ye shall be free indeed" (John 8:36). It is easier, however, to rail against an "evil establishment" and forget one's own evil nature than to recognize that the only freedom is under God and His law, and unredeemed men, as slaves of sin, can only create a slave society.

Chapter Four
Feasts and Holy Times

1. The Sabbath: Genesis 2:2-3; Exodus 20:8-11; Deuteronomy 5:12-15; Exodus 23:12; 34:21; 35:2; Amos 8:5; Jeremiah 17:21-22; Leviticus 19:3, 30; 23:3; 26:2; Numbers 15:32-36; 28:9-10; Exodus 16:22-26; 35:1-3; 31:12-17.

2. The Passover: Exodus 12:1-14, 25-27, 43-48; 34:25; Deuteronomy 16:1-8.

3. Unleavened bread: Exodus 12:1-20, 43-50; 13:3-10; 23:14-15; 34:18; Leviticus 23:4-8; Deuteronomy 16:3-4, 8; Joshua 5:10; 2 Chronicles 30:5-9; 35:6; Numbers 9:1-14; 28:16-25. *Excommunication* for refusal to celebrate, Numbers 9:13.

4. Feast of Weeks, First Fruits: Exodus 23:14-16; 34:22; Leviticus 23:15-21; Numbers 28:26-31; Deuteronomy 16:9-12.

5. Feast of Tabernacles, or Ingathering: Exodus 23:16; 34:22; Leviticus 23:33-36, 39-43; Deuteronomy 16:13-17; Ezra 3:4; 1 Kings 8:2; 2 Chronicles 5:3; Numbers 29:12-38.

6. Sabbatical Year: Exodus 23:10-12; Deuteronomy 15:1-2; Leviticus 25:1-5, 20-22; Jeremiah 34:12-16.

7. New Moon: Numbers 28:11-15; Ezekiel 46:3.

8. Atonement: Exodus 30:10; Leviticus 16:1-22, 26-32; 25:9; Numbers 29:7-11.

9. Trumpets: Leviticus 23:23-25; Numbers 29:1-6; 10:10.

10. Year of Jubilee: Leviticus 25:8-16, 23-34, 39-42, 47-52, 54.

11. Males must worship thrice yearly on the three major feasts: Exodus 23:17; 34:23; Deuteronomy 16:16.

Two notable facts must be commented on here: these are the religious observances commanded by God of the covenant people. However, *first*, it must be noted that while failure to observe the Passover requires the excommunication of the man who has no valid excuse for his failure (Num. 9:13), we have on the whole an attitude of forbearance. *Second*, the religious days in the calendar are seen as feasts and as privileged participations, not as penalties. The man who observes God's feasts and holy days is neither restricted nor penalized thereby but privileged and blessed. The perspective thus is not of a penalizing inclusion but a privileged participation. This is far from the attitude of one mother I once heard tell her children, "I had to suffer through Sunday school and church, and you are going to do it too, for your own good!"

Thus, non-participation is its own penalty on the whole. The excommunication for refusal to celebrate the Passover simply confirms the folly

15

of the man who cuts himself off from the atonement and chooses his own way of life and deliverance.

Those who reject God and the means of grace are fools. Their future is to be outside of God and His Kingdom. The word for *hell* (Gehenna, or Hinnom) refers to the city dump, a place of junk and trash, of decay and worms, and of fires to consume the piles of waste. Anyone who chooses the garbage dump over God is someone to separate ourselves from.

The Sabbath means *rest.* It means the confidence that our future is not in our hands but God's, that He is the absolute Lord and determiner. Luther rightfully trusted in the words of the psalmist rather than his own limited foreknowledge when he declared, "I shall not die, but live, and declare the words of the LORD" (Ps. 118:17). To rest in the Lord means to take hands off our lives and to commit them to God's providence and care. To live without resting in the Lord is to make hell our residence and troubles our unending companion.

To rest from our labors, as God rested from His (Gen. 2:2), does not mean inactivity necessarily, but sitting back in the knowledge of a glorious accomplishment, God's Kingdom work.

Quite rightly, the Sabbath has been a day of song and of singing because it is a day of triumph. It is a foretaste of the fulness of victory and peace. Those who turn the Sabbath rest into a time of solemn misery desecrate the Sabbath.

The Passover means deliverance. The Hebrew Sabbath commemorates Israel's deliverance; the Christian Sabbath celebrates the Christian's victory in and through Christ over the power of sin and death. "Christ our Passover is sacrificed for us" (1 Cor. 5:7).

The feasts of Unleavened Bread, of Weeks, and of Tabernacles, have been absorbed into other days of the Christian calendar, but their spirit lives in true thanksgiving and worship.

The sabbatical year again was a privilege. It marked a time of prolonged rest, and of release from debt. It meant no long term debts, no more than for six years. When and where observed by Christians, it meant debt-free living as the normal way of life, and a year-long rest for man and for the earth. Man is the loser for embracing long-term debt, and he is the loser for refusing true rest. According to Isaiah 57:20-21,

> 20. But the wicked are like the troubled sea, when it cannot rest, whose waters cast up mire and dirt.
> 21. There is no peace, saith my God, to the wicked.

Men talk of wanting peace, but they hate it because it brings them face to face with their emptiness. To be in conflict gives them a sense of empty purpose and a way of evading God.

The new moon was another religious occasion. The celebration of time is a *religious* event. For fallen, unregenerate man, the passage of time means aging, decay, and death. For the man of God, it means that God's purposes have been advanced, because all things are in His sovereign power. We are to view time, therefore, not simply in personal terms but rather as God's advancement of His victory. If we make ourselves a part of His purpose, we are then a part of His triumph.

The atonement, is, of course, central to our faith because it accomplishes our restoration into God's calling and Kingdom. The atonement tells us that God's justice requires restitution. Where there is no restitution, there is no justice. The legal systems of Christendom for centuries rested on the doctrine of the atonement; as they depart from it, they falter and fail.

The feast of trumpets was observed on the first day of the seventh month. In Exodus 19:16-19, the voice of God on Sinai was preceded by a great blast of trumpets that terrified the people. The trumpet sound was thus an "image" of the voice of God (Rev. 1:10; 4:1). The trumpet is a herald of power and of war and of the presence of majesty.

This is why the year of Jubilee was proclaimed by trumpets (Lev. 25:9). The Jubilee year was a time of restoration. Faithfulness to the sabbatical years made a society free of long-term debt and free from a boom-and-bust cycle. It provided for the restoration of the soil's fertility by rest, and it maintained the stability and continuity of rural society. The Jubilee year was basic to the pattern of life required by God. Important as it was and is, no law allowed man to enforce it. God, Himself, punishes the lawless societies.

Men had to take the leadership in worship, and their visits to the sanctuary thrice annually set forth the responsibility of men towards God. Since the Enlightenment in particular, worship has been left too often to women and children.

What we see is that in these laws, given much space in the books of law, *only one* is enforceable by man. The surrender of enforcement in many areas by man to God is mandatory. His laws must be enforced according to His requirements. For church or state to assume the power of enforcement in these areas is to claim to be as God. To attempt to punish men where God's law gives no permission to do so is to play God, something not taken lightly by the Almighty. When and where is it written that God added church or state to the Trinity and gave them independent powers to enforce His laws where not required to do so by Him?

The Lord God can run the world very well without man's unasked for help. Men are too prone to disobey God by neglecting His requirements and then trying to play God in areas where God gives them no jurisdiction.

The transgression of jurisdiction is sometimes more serious than the transgression of a particular law because it transfers to man, or to the church or state, powers rightly and exclusively the prerogative of God. In Matthew 21:31, our Lord said to the religious and civil leaders of His day, "Verily I say unto you,

That the publicans and the harlots go into the Kingdom of God before you." There is no reason to believe that He has since changed His mind about hypocrisy, Phariseeism, and claims to illegitimate powers.

Chapter Five
Circumcision

Thus far and yet further, the subjects considered are ones of indifference to modern man, and they probably bring a yawn to his face. It will have to be granted that the Bible makes clear that they are important to God. One would therefore expect God to view neglect, for example, of circumcision, and later of baptism, very seriously *and* impose penalties for neglect.

We see circumcision required in Genesis 17:9-14, 21:4; Exodus 12:48 and Leviticus 12:3. Circumcision is the sign of the covenant, of God's treaty with His people. But failure to be circumcised had no penalty *except* to bar one from the passover (Ex. 12:48). This was, of course, a bar from membership and office in the redeemed nation. God clearly did not trust men to punish a disregard for His covenant. This is a very important fact that tells us much about God's government. Where men will thunder threats and kill, God keeps His silence. The penalties of separating ourselves from Him are usually enough.

The circumcision of the male child was on the eighth day. In the early church, eighth-day baptism was practiced for a time.

More importantly, the child was not allowed to come of age and then decide on circumcision, or later, baptism. Salvation is not by man's choice but by God's choice, and therefore the rites or ordinances of circumcision and baptism make clear in practice that the choice is God's not a child's. The parents give their child to the Lord with the promise to rear the child in the covenant of grace and law. The rest is up to God.

The Bible is a *covenant* book; it tells us of the covenant grace and law. This is the key connection between God and man, His covenant. All the same, He allows us to attach no penalties to our failure to rely on His grace and law.

Men have trouble keeping their hands off anything they control. Rome insisted on giving citizenship to every man in the empire, and it thereby made citizenship, *first*, worthless, and *second*, a burden because it was accompanied by total controls. Now democracies are moving suicidally towards requiring everyone to vote, including criminals.

If baptism is made universal, it is meaningless. God's wisdom most certainly exceeds that of man!

Chapter Six
Taxation

The subject of taxation is very important to most men because the exactions of civil governments are so oppressive. The modern humanistic state sees itself, as did the ancient pagan state, as the basic and ultimate power. It holds that it has the "right" to tax, confiscate, or seize properties and assets at will. Its premise is the antithesis of Psalm 24:1, "The earth is the LORD'S and the fulness thereof; the world, and they that dwell therein." Statism holds that the earth, its assets, and its peoples belong to the state, directly or indirectly. Its power to tax includes its power to take over everything within its borders.

As scholars study the Bible, they try to find in it whatever conforms to their idea of the state. Thus, one scholar has seen 2 Samuel 24:1ff., and 1 Chronicles 27:23, 24, as a census for tax purposes. But taxation is never mentioned in the text! In 1 Kings 5:13, we have an account of Solomon's tax on men, their forced labor, but this is by no means a part of God's law. On the contrary, God through Samuel tells Israel by disobeying Him and by turning to a human king, they will be punished by the royal tax, forced labor among other things (1 Sam. 8:10-18). In fact, Samuel says that one of the evils of a monarchy will be a 10 percent tax! (1 Sam. 8:15, 17) The taxation of "the land" at the demand of Pharaoh in 2 Kings 23:35 is a form of oppression, not God's law.

The civil tax in God's law is given in Exodus 30:11-16. It applies to all males from 20 years old and above. It is to be the same for all, rich and poor alike. "The rich shall not give more, and the poor shall not give less than half a shekel" (v. 15). Equal taxation is required.

This tax is "to make an atonement for your souls" (vv. 15-16). This seems to indicate that this was a *religious* tax, and rightly so, because "church," "state," family, society, and more were all religious in terms of God's law. We know that early in the Christian era this tax was paid by Jesus to the Jewish Patriarch or Prince of Palestine, who used it to govern and regulate civil matters that concerned Jews, insofar as Roman law allowed.[1] When Jewish princedoms arose, as in Narbonne and Septimania, this poll tax was paid to their Patriarch or *nasi*, prince.[2] This was a Davidic line.

Clearly, this poll tax was the civil tax, and the only legitimate one. Curiously, scholars are unwilling to admit this. It would mark the godly state as an extremely limited one. At the same time, the Temple or priestly tithe was only one percent of the believer's tithe, which was paid to the Levites (Num. 18:26). This was used by the Levites to provide a variety of services, care of the

---

[1.] Arthur J. Zuckerman, *A Jewish Princedom in Feudal France, 768-900* (New York, N.Y.: Columbia University Press, (1965) 1972), p. 3.
[2.] *ibid.*, p. 93, 112ff.

sanctuary, its music, service as educators, judges, and more. God does not in His law permit a rich and powerful state nor church.

Those who see a broader tax do so by appealing to the violations of God's law cited by Samuel rather than to the law itself. Thus, the *Encyclopaedia Judaica* (vol. 15, p. 840) sees 1 Samuel 8:10ff. as giving the state a tithe of the taxes enumerated by Samuel.

Daniel C. Snell has stated, "Taxation is extremely important to the state, and the state cannot be said to exist in it fullest form if it has not taxing power."[3] Exactly so, and this tells us why God's law does not permit a power state or church.

It is important to note that this tax is a head or poll tax on *males* 20 and over in age. It is not a tax on land nor on anything else. Certainly it is not a tax on the Temple. We see the Biblical position clearly in the rescript gained from Artaxerxes of Persia. It exempted the Temple, everything in it, "the priests and Levites, singers, porters, Nethenims, or minister of this house of God" from taxation; "it shall not be lawful to impose toll, tribute, or custom, upon them" (Ezra 7:24). The rescript (Ezra 7:11-26) provided a summary of the strictly limited perspective of the law, and a model in later conflicts with overlords.

The Biblical requirement is thus for a very severely limited state and church, restricted in its income to prevent it from becoming powerful and oppressive. The central source of government must be the man over 20, who by his self-government under God provides the basic unit of rule. Where the person is weak, state and church become powerful and tyrannical.

There is no evading the force of God's law here. Those who deny the application of Exodus 30:11-16 must then say that God gave no taxing power to the state, or else that at this point God left all taxing power to the state. Either way, we have God abdicating His royal power, an absurd conclusion.

The modern church and state thus have good reasons to hate God's law because it limits their power and their government. God's law here directs clearly to the adult males as the governing center, each in their own area. The antinomians are pronomians where the laws of church and state, man-made laws, are concerned. Church and state have both done some good over the centuries, but at the price of man's freedom and responsibility. The world around us is full of irresponsible and unfree men because they prefer slavery and taxation over faith and freedom.

---

[3] Daniel C. Snell, "Taxes and Taxation," in David Noel Freeman, general editor: *The Anchor Bible Dictionary*, vol. 6 (New York, N.Y.: Doubleday, 1992), p. 338.

Chapter Seven
The Courts

1. Courts held at the city gates: Deuteronomy 21:19; 22:15; 25:7.

2. Court of appeals: Exodus 18:26.

A court is a place of settlement of disputes and punishment of offenses and crimes. The offenses, crimes, sins, and various transgressions are defined by the law of the land; law in turn is the moral expression of a religion. There is no neutral law; law by its very nature is against all violations and transgressions of the fundamental religious premises of the country. As a result, law-systems vary. There are major differences between the law-systems of various religions, e.g., Shintoism, Buddhism, Hinduism, humanism, Mohammedanism, etc., and Christianity. It is naive when not perverse for humanists to believe that their law-system is the one true structure, especially when they deny that an absolute truth exists.

The presuppositions of a culture determine its laws. If the God of Scripture be our starting point, then we have a very different system of laws than do the humanists. For the Christian, if he believes the Bible, God's law is the only definition of justice. For the humanist, man's developing awareness of his existentialist being, and the relative nature of all things, defines law for him, or tentatively so.

When the political order, its courts, and its schools, are controlled by humanists, the legal system with its structures will be logically and progressively anti-Christian. Christianity is then in fact a threat to the humanist society because it posits and requires a radically different law order.

Rome might have felt that Isis "worship," or Mithraism, were cults unworthy of Romans, but both were accepted because both had only superficial differences in their man-centered, "consumer-centered" character. Christianity, on the other hand, challenged the very premises of Roman civil government and society.

Where courts represent the will of the ruler, then the court becomes increasingly withdrawn from God and man. Courtrooms built in the 1980s in the U.S. increasingly limited the space available to the people, to as little as 24 persons in one instance. Neither the victim nor the public have as much place in the proceedings as the state itself, and the state's minions command most of the space now.

God's law is given to all the people, and therefore the court is held at the city gates where the proceedings in antiquity were most public. It was thus truly an *open court*. God's law, in a godly society, would be openly taught and would be known by all the people. The proceedings thus would reveal whether or not the civil authorities were faithful to God's law and not those of the king, or some other man. God Himself in Joel 3:12 speaks of a public judgment upon an ungodly people.

In antiquity, courts in many cultures were held at the gate of the city, or in front of the temple, and, later, at a large judgment hall. As power was concentrated in the hands of a ruler, the court was moved into his chambers or palace because it was *his* law and *his* court.

Our very word *court* reflects a strange history. *Court* comes from the Latin *cohors, cors*, which is akin to *hors, hort, hortus*, a garden, and it means an enclosed area. We can go a step further to point out that a *court* is thus a private area, not a public one as in the Biblical judgment place.

We can therefore say that the law and its courts have gone from being a totally God-centered and public matter to a private domain of a state and its professional class. Now both law and the courts are defined by the state and increasingly anti-Christian.

Curiously, at the same time the state has redefined religion, Christianity is being relegated to the private domain, and the state to the public. As a purely private concern, Christianity, it is held, cannot legitimately seek to influence the public domain. This in effect denies Christianity the right to exist. If it be no more than a purely private concern, it can no more seek to influence the public sphere than can a stamp collectors' club, even less so.

God's law is for all men and nations, and its jurisdiction is determined in all cases by God and His word. Because God is the Creator of heaven and earth and all things therein, nothing is outside or beyond His government. For anyone or any agency to seek to limit God's law, or to supplant it with their own, is to try to be God (Gen. 3:5) and to replace God. This is certainly a way of invoking God's judgment!

The *enclosure*, the modern court, now eliminates increasingly God above all else, and it thereby excludes *justice*. *Just* and *justice* are increasingly defined as conformity to *fact* or to *reason*. Justice Holmes objected to law as logic in favor of law as experience. The law as God's word of justice was not even considered by him. The law as the distillation of human experience is a very shallow thing. Modern legal positivism is strongly in agreement with the position of Thomas Hobbes, who in his *Leviathan* said,

> To the care of the Sovereign, belongeth the making of Good Lawes. But what is a Good Law? By a Good Law, I mean not a Just Law: for no law can be unjust. The Law is made by the Sovereign Power, and all that is done by such Power, is warranted, and owned by everyone of the people; and that which every man will have so, no man can say is unjust. It is the Lawes of a Commonwealth, as in the Lawes of Gaming: whatsoever the Gamesters all agree on, is injustice to none of them. A good Law is that, which is Needful, for the Good of the People, and withall Perspicuous.[1]

Rousseau was in the air long before his time. Despite his dissimilarities to Hobbes, both were in a common tradition. Hobbes, *first* of all, sees no law as unjust. This is an amazing statement, certainly for a man of his time. *Second*, a law is the will of the sovereign power, for him the king. *Third*, the people give assent to the law, but how in a kingdom of Hobbes' day could they veto it? *Fourth*, he uses the analogy of a gambling game, wherein all gamblers give assent to the rules. But at times to my knowledge gambling games have been crooked, and no one has objected because one man has a knife or a gun in his hand. Does this make the game honest? The modern state makes the law, and dissent is beyond the ability of most people.

When Pilate said to Jesus, "What is truth?" (John 18:38), he was probably not the first, and certainly not the last judge, to express contempt or doubt concerning truth and justice.

From non-Christian courts, what else can we expect? And, given the fact of man's fallen nature, it is difficult enough to expect justice from "Christian" courts, but we have no other hope, and we must work patiently and faithfully to establish godly courts.

Because the court is God-ordained, it must represent God and His law, not man. Justice is God's concern, whereas fallen men seek their advantage. Redeemed men are sinful still, and they cannot be trusted to represent anything other than God and His law, and then cautiously and with checks and balances. Because man's basic desire and his original sin is to be his own god and to determine for himself what is good and evil, law and morality, man is dangerous when left to his own devices.

Courts are now a part of the state and its bureaucracy. In 1 Corinthians 6:1ff., the court St. Paul requires, in terms of God and His law, is made up of godly men, but it is neither an aspect of church or state but the representative of God's justice. In 1 Corinthians 6:9-10, St. Paul makes clear that the unrighteous or unjust, *the ungodly*, shall not inherit the Kingdom of God. How then can they administer God's justice? How can men who are unrighteous, fornicators, idolaters, adulterers, effeminate, homosexuals or sodomites, covetous men, drunkards, revilers, or extortioners, "inherit the kingdom of God"? Such men cannot administer justice because justice is only possible by means of God's law. To expect justice from the ungodly is to expect grapes from thorns (Matt. 7:16).

Geoffrey Norman has described the radical injustice common to U. S. administrative courts. The Environmental Protection Agency charges men but allows no defense, only a guilty plea. Norman reports on the case of an environmentalist, dedicated to cleaning up pollution, who was taken to court by an agency created by Vice-President Al Gore to "save" the environment. Men so charged, Biff Mithoffer said,

---

[1.] Thomas Hobbes: *Leviathan* (London, England: J.M. Dent, Everyman Library; (1651) 1937), p. 185.

...don't have any of those rights. (The right of a criminal to face his accuser and to be judged by a jury of his peers.) PRPs (Potentially Responsible Parties) don't. Criminals get specific punishments. So many years in jail. A PRP's sentence lasts until the EPA (Environmental Protections Agency) is tired of screwing with him, or figures there isn't any blood left.[2]

The more recently created the court, as of the 1990s, the further it is from God and justice. A return to justice will not come with a change of presidents and members of Congress but only with a return to the God of Scripture. We have abandoned God's Savior and God's law. As a result, we have been importing hell from eternity into time.

---

[2] Geoffrey Norman, "Superfund as Godzilla," in *The American Spectator*, Vol. 26, no. 11, November, 1993, pp. 38-43.

Chapter Eight
The Judges

1. Judges and their duty: Deuteronomy 16:18-20; 1:16; 19:15-19; 25:1-2.

2. The character of judges: Exodus 23:6-8; Leviticus 19:15; 24:22.

3. The Supreme Judge: Genesis 18:25.

4. The priests as interpreters of God's law: Deuteronomy 21:5.

From Deuteronomy 21:5, we learn that priests had a part in the court as interpreters of God's law. These men could be priests or Levites, according to Josephus.[1] Each judge, according to Josephus, had two Levites assigned to him to assist him by determining what law or laws of God applied to the case at hand. This did not mean rendering the decision of *guilty* or *innocent*, but establishing which law or laws of God applied to the case at hand, the nature of the penalty, and so on. The judges who heard all such cases governed the proceedings and rendered the decision, but the Levites expounded the relevant law.

This requirement is essentially tied to the law set forth in Deuteronomy 1:17:

> Ye shall not respect persons in judgments; but ye shall hear the small as well as the great; ye shall not be afraid of the face of man; for the judgment is God's.

God is the Supreme Judge of all men and nations, and He requires all to obey His law. He has not relinquished His right to rule to any other, nor does He recognize as law any law other than His own. It is an offensive act to call the Lord *God* while denying His law.

No "respect of persons in judgment" (Deut. 1:17) does not mean impartiality because its premise is a partiality to God and His law, to justice, rather than to men. The law is totally against evil-doers, criminals, but their guilt must be determined before sentence is passed. Until then, there must be a careful attention to evidence.

In Exodus 23:6-8, the judge is, *first*, forbidden to "tamper with a poor man's rights in court," in Moffatt's rendering. *Second*, false charges are to be avoided, because innocent persons are greatly damaged thereby, even when acquitted. *Third*, innocent peoples must not be put to death, nor bad men acquitted. *Fourth*, bribes must never be accepted because they destroy the cases of good men, and they blind justice.

The judge must represent God, and the term *elohim*, gods, is even applied to judges because they function for God and His law, or should (Ps. 82:6). God required that judges be appointed in all the cities (Deut. 16:18), together with priests and Levites to work with them (Deut. 17:8ff; 19:8f.).

---

[1] *Antiquities of the Jews*, Book IV, viii.

In Exodus 21:22, the judge seems to be given discretion with respect to the sentence. It is to be "as the judges determine," but what it means is that the penalty must be in terms of the damages, and this is clearly stated in the following verses, Exodus 21:23-25.

God requires, as Leviticus 24:22 makes plain, "one manner of law, as well for the stranger, as for one of your own country: for I am the LORD your God." Only under Biblical law is there equal justice. In other religions, the concept of justice is an alien one. When I was young, I heard a missionary tell of an experience in an East Asian country. One morning, one of the missionary's very young sons was playing with other boys from local families. The boys picked up pebbles and tossed them at one peasant's cow. Later that day, the cow died. It had long been ill and close to death. A village court found the missionary's son guilty, but none of the native boys. The penalty was a new cow for the peasant. When the missionary protested, the villagers were both astonished that he did, and also angry. Had he no sense of justice, no knowledge of right and wrong? After all, he had two cows, and the peasant now had none.

Such concepts of justice are commonplace outside of Biblical faith. They have arisen rapidly in the Western world even as Christianity has receded. If the judge's religion is man-centered, his idea of justice will be also. If the judge be man-centered, his decisions will seek to please men and not God.

If a judge represents church, state, or any other agency, he will be unjust and partial because he will represent an institution, however good, rather than God the Lord, the true lawgiver.

Judge Harold J. Rothwax has rightly observed, "We know from our history that we have to control government. The American Revolution arose from that belief."[2] Judges too need to be "controlled," but the basic control is self-control. If men do not believe in God's justice and law, they are then not under the control of anything but their self-will, whether they be judges, pastors and priests, or laymen generally. The history of crime is the history of man's self-will, his firm belief that life is best if "my will be done."

---

[2] Harold J. Rothwax, *Guilty: The Collapse of Criminal Justice* (New York, N.Y.: Random House, 1996), p. 32.

Chapter Nine

Appeals

1. The first appeals were to Moses: Deuteronomy 1:17; Exodus 18:26.

2. Later, they were to the priests: Deuteronomy 17:8-12; 19:17.

In later history, in Israel, appeals were to the king (2 Sam. 14:4-11; 1 Kings 3:16). Still later, in Christ's time, they were to the Sanhedrin.

The premise that undergirds and requires courts of appeal is man's sin and fallibility. If we assume that the best men are our judges, we must still take their status as men for granted, not all-wise, not sinless, and not infallible.

In both church and state, this elementary premise is gone. Appellate courts are no longer concerned with reviewing the case in terms of its rightness or wrongness but only in terms of its procedural correctness. Churches that claim to be orthodox refuse to reconsider a case as to whether or not justice prevailed, but only to see if proper procedures are followed. This means the lowest court can commit flagrant injustice, and be sustained in it, provided the procedure is correct.

The review of appellate courts in church and state thus rests on a peculiar premise. *First*, by refusing to examine a case as to whether or not injustice prevailed, the courts of appeal assume the infallibility of the lowest court. *Second*, by accepting a case on appeal, they assume that a procedural mistake occurred! How can a decision be immune to appeal on the grounds of injustice and yet subject to retrial on procedural grounds? Often the procedural grounds involve trifles, nothing relating to justice.

Such a state of affairs is only possible when justice is no longer essential, and only "the dignity of the court" matters.

It is not at all surprising that this change from justice to procedure has coincided with the growth of the modern power state. It makes the modern power state immune to the technical status of fallibility but preserves it intact in its arrogant autonomy.

The courts in this perverse state deny at the same time any higher law and the God who gave that law. They thereby deny that any law or morality exists above and over the state whereby the state can and must be judged. The rejection of God enables the state to play God.

Not surprisingly, the older system of local, county, state, and federal courts has steadily given way to bureaucratic courts. This does not mean that the older system, now radically humanistic, is good, simply that the new bureaucratic courts are more efficient in their tyranny.

The choice is always between God and tyranny, although sometimes, given man's tyranny, we get tyranny in the name of God and justice. When we get such an evil state, we have an obligation to work for justice by prayerfully working to restore all men and institutions to their rightful place under God and His Christ.

In Deuteronomy 17:8-12, it is important to note that, on appeal, priests and Levites are to take part in the proceedings as well as the judges. Because justice is a moral and religious fact, the presence of experts in God's law is a necessity. The meaning of an appeal is gone when justice is not a moral consideration.

Because of the Christian impact on the whole world, even Marxist nations have ostensible appellate courts. These, however, are unconcerned with justice and their function is a facade whereby the form is observed and the substance gutted.

In Luke 18:3, we read of a helpless widow's cry to a judge, "Avenge me of mine adversary." This is a cry resounding over the centuries in millions of voices. Even worse, churches which should uphold the sovereign and triune God and His law deny that law. By doing so, they have joined the unjust judge and are adversaries of Jesus Christ.

Chapter Ten
Witnesses and Evidence

1. The oath: Exodus 22:10-11; Leviticus 6:1-7.

2. Witnesses to criminal acts must testify to what they have seen: Leviticus 5:1.

3. In murder cases, two witnesses are required for conviction: Numbers 35:30; Deuteronomy 17:6-7; 19:15. This same requirement applies to all cases: Deuteronomy 19:15.

4. Collusion "with the wicked to be an unrighteous witness" is forbidden: Exodus 23:1.

5. The witness must back up his testimony by assisting in the execution: Deuteronomy 17:7.

6. Perjury is forbidden: Exodus 20:16; 23:1; Leviticus 19:12; Deuteronomy 5:20; 19:16-21.

7. The penalty for false witness is that the possible penalty for the accused becomes the penalty of the perjured witness: Deuteronomy 19:16-21.

8. The law of evidences is cited by Paul as a general premise of judgment: "In the mouth of two or three witnesses shall every word be established," 2 Corinthians 13:1.

Justice cannot prevail without honest and conscientious witnesses, because the witnesses provide the evidence necessary for correct judgments by a court. In any society where perjury is not punished, justice soon disappears. At present, in the U. S. and elsewhere, perjury is rarely punished, and, as a result, justice is beginning to disappear.

The English word *witness* goes back to Old English and Gothic, to a root, *wit*, meaning to observe, or to know. In the Old English, it is *witnes*, knowledge, testimony, and the word is associated with an *oath*. Its legal connotation has a long history.

Judges hear a case, but it is the witnesses who in effect present the case with their testimony. Circumstantial evidence is a form of witness.

Biblical law states that witnesses have a moral and religious obligation to testify to what they know (Lev. 5:1). Community life requires all men to further justice by testifying to what they know or have seen. Community cannot exist unless men see it as their obligation to uphold justice even when it militates against them. In Deuteronomy 21:18-21, we have a law that requires the death penalty for habitual criminals. In such cases, the parents must testify against their son and give evidence to his lawless life as an habitual criminal offender. This is an unusual requirement because it requires the family of the incorrigible criminal to side with God's law and not in favor of a family member. Justice, not blood, must govern their stand.

By analogy, we cannot allow race or nationality to blind us to justice. The "stranger" or alien must not be oppressed, legally or socially (Ex. 22:21; 23:9; Lev. 19:33; 25:35; Deut. 10:18-19). This is a law echoed by the psalms and the prophets and is a fundamental aspect of Biblical morality. Widows and orphans are similarly protected. The just society is thus both godly and neighborly.

This is clearly related to the laws of witness because we are not morally allowed to be selective in our witnessing, nor in our community life, nor in our justice. Hence the modern oath still echoes this requirement in calling for "the whole truth, and nothing but the truth." We are not to be judges by our witnessing, but we thereby make possible true judgment.

The witness makes justice possible. This is an important fact because once again we see that it is not the people "at the top" who make possible a good society but the people at large. It is easy to rail at corrupt courts, but our problem is as often a corrupt people who will not testify to the truth.

I was young when I first saw a witness perjure himself for his own advantage. The unwillingness to witness to the truth is now commonplace. Men cannot complain of injustices when they are a party to it, as too many are today.

Chapter Eleven
The Sentence

1. Restitution: Numbers 5:6-7; Exodus 21:12, 22-27; 22:1-15; Leviticus 24:18-21.

2. Death Penalty: Genesis 9:6; Exodus 21:12, 14; Leviticus 24:17.

3. Corporal punishment: Deuteronomy 25:2-3.

The law system of God's word has no place for imprisonment except temporary retention pending a trial. If found guilty, the man could be subjected to three kinds of sentences. *First*, in minor offenses, there could be a sentence of corporal punishment, a public beating before the court and the people (Deut. 25:1-3). No more than forty stripes could be administered, lest "thy brother should seem vile to thee." Punishment, not abject degradation, was in mind.

Second, in most cases, restitution was required, i.e., a restoration of what was taken, or its equivalent, plus an additional amount. The additional amount could be up to five fold, depending on the nature of the offense. In Exodus 22, we see that the restitution had to be, in most cases, the equivalent of double the value. However, oxen were valuable for their trained status as beasts of burden, pulling wagons, plows, etc., and they were also valued for their hide and meat. Their restitution price was "five oxen for an ox," whereas sheep were "four sheep for a sheep" (Ex. 22:1). Sheep had a high value as food, as a source of wool, and because of their reproductive potential.

Most offenses required restitution in kind or an equivalent value.

Third, the death penalty was a form of restitution. It did not exclude the necessity for restitution where this was necessary, but in all cases where required the death penalty was mandatory.

Fourth, if an offender when convicted could not make restitution, he could then be sentenced to bond-service for a time in order to work out his restitution. Texts that speak of this include Exodus 21:2-6, Deuteronomy 24:14f., and 15:12-15. These texts indicate that the bondservant could be sold to someone who needed his labor when the man who won the judgment needed an immediate recompense. In any event, the bondservant had to be treated as a brother, not as a slave. The maximum term of a bondservant was six years. Neither debt, nor involuntary servitude, could go beyond the sabbath year of rest in the Lord.

The premise of these laws is restitution towards a restoration of godly order. All God's laws are aspects of the creation mandate of Genesis 1:26-28, the establishment of God's order by, *first*, obedience to His laws of righteousness or justice, and, *second*, by extending the boundaries of God's rule over evil-doers and thereby making them serve His Kingdom.

Ungodly sentences penalize the law-abiding by requiring them to maintain in prisons at great cost all criminals who are convicted. A professional criminal class is developed, so that the godly are required to support the ungodly and see them increase.

Fifth, in Deuteronomy 21:18-21, a law long part of American law, the habitual criminal was executed. A permanent criminal class was thereby avoided. For at least the first half of the 20th century, in most American states, a criminal, either on his third or fourth conviction, depending on the state, was ruled to be an habitual criminal and sentenced to death. Humanism in the courts has overturned this premise and led to the creation of a growing criminal class. Sympathy for criminals has led to an indifference in many quarters to the plight of victims.

Law cannot be neutral. It condemns some and protects others. The issue is, whom does the law protect, and who gets disfavor from the law? The law can protect the state, the law-breaker, or the law-abiding peoples who are victimized. It is clearly apparent that, in the latter part of the 20th century, the law has been protecting the state above the people. At the same time, the decisions of the U. S. Supreme Court have demonstrated an arrogant unconcern for the people and have favored the criminal to an increasing degree.

The *sentence* of the court is, where godly, the first line of defense of a people. Occasionally, sometimes frequently, there are wars between nations, sometimes over trifling political reasons, sometimes to forestall aggression and invasion. These are normally occasional although still too frequent and costly. There is, however, a constant around the clock warfare by the lawless in a society against the law-abiding. In this warfare, the police are relatively helpless because the courts and their sentences constitute the primary line of defense. This perpetual war of the lawless against society is lost when the sympathies of courts and juries are with the lawless.

Because the present legal system permits it, Christians are commonly excluded from juries. One lawyer, not a Christian, observed, "The only way now that you can get a jury of your peers is to be a skid row character." Increasingly, good men and women ask to be excluded from jury duty because they know that after a day of waiting, they will not be picked. Some have commented that, *if they had the money*, they would challenge the premises of exclusion whereby professional men, businessmen, the clergy, and others of moral stature are routinely excluded.

The background of the jury system is related to the nature of witnesses, i.e., judgment in its broader sense coming from the community of God's people.

At one time in U. S. history, no man could be a witness unless he could take an oath religiously, as a Christian. Some judges would allow an unbeliever to testify without an oath, but they would then warn the jury that the man's word was not worth much since there was no fear of God in him. Now there is no fear of God even in churchmen when under oath. There is thus a rottenness in the bones of the legal system.

Chapter Twelve

Execution

1. The witnesses participated in the execution of the condemned man: Deuteronomy 17:7.

2. Only the condemned man, not his family, was punished: Deuteronomy 24:16.

As we have seen, the witness, if he were dishonest and was caught in his perjury, had to suffer the exact penalty which would have been imposed on the man on trial. There was a severe penalty for perjury. If the man were convicted, the witnesses had to participate in his actual execution, to back up their testimony with action. In fact, the whole community had to be involved in the execution (Deut. 17:7). It was their community that was at stake. The use of stoning was not a mandatory aspect of the law, simply one form of the death penalty among others. For some time in American law, community members were present as a way of giving assent to the sentence of the law.

Punishment was limited to the offender, or offenders, not to the family or relatives unless they were involved in the offense. In the case of Achan, we see, *first*, that his confession was not enough to convict him. There had to be corroboration. *Second*, the stolen items were found in his tent, and under it, which meant that his family was also guilty, and therefore was killed (Joshua 7:22-25).

Deuteronomy 24:16 summarized this premise of the law:

> The fathers shall not be put to death for the children, neither shall the children be put to death for the fathers: every man shall be put to death for his own sin.

This law has been commonly disregarded by the nations. During much of Western history, acts, sentences, or bills of attainder, punished the family of a guilty man, usually a traitor, by seizing all his assets and properties and forfeiting all claims by his wife and family to them. Such measures are forbidden by the U. S. Constitution but are still common practice. For example, the U. S. Internal Revenue Service does seize funds of the entire family, or their properties, when they are not involved in the father's offense, or the wife is separated, or even divorced. This kind of injustice tells us how far from justice humanistic law systems are.

Deuteronomy 24:16 speaks of the death penalty being applicable only to the offender. By analogy, of course, it includes all offenses, capital or otherwise. As Ezekiel 18:4 sums it up, "the soul that sinneth, it shall die."

God declares that *the land* itself is polluted by man's sin and spues out an ungodly people. The weather and the land work against evil peoples (Lev. 18:24-30; Deut. 28:1ff.), even as it also blesses the godly. God brings about His sentence of execution by using the forces of nature against a people. If a people will not cleanse themselves of the ungodly, God will cleanse His earth of these peoples. Our task of cleansing cannot be a lawless one but must be accomplished by conversion, and then by instruction in God's law- word.

Chapter Thirteen
Offenses Against Justice

1. Bribery is the subversion of justice: Exodus 23:8; Deuteronomy 16:19; 24:17 (Ps. 26:10; Isa. 1:23; etc.).

2. Perjury, bearing false witness, is the subversion of justice: Leviticus 19:12; Exodus 20:16; Deuteronomy 19:16-19 (Prov. 25:18; 19:5, 9).

We have already seen that perjury is a very serious offense against God and man. Now we must see that bribery is similarly serious. Both are attempted subversions of God's order. There can be no just order where bribery and perjury prevail. They constitute the murder of justice. Therefore, the punishment of perjury is *mandatory* (Deut. 19:16-19). The judges have a duty to investigate the testimony made before them to ascertain its truth, and to punish the offender "as he had thought to have done unto his brother: so shalt thou put the evil away from among you" (Deut. 19:19). There must be no pity for a man who attempts to frustrate justice: in fact, the court's judgment must create fear among men and serve as a means to prevent others from the same offense.

To buy the court's favor by money is to strike at God: the judge then has betrayed his trust.

An offense against justice is an offense against God whose law is subverted. A judge who accepts a bribe or tolerates perjury is as guilty as the offender. The subversion of justice is an offense against God and His court and therefore a great evil. Bribery is called, in Deuteronomy 16:19, wresting or tampering with justice, and the perversion thereof.

Because the *law* is the Lord's, and *justice* is the expression of His being, any offense against justice is directly against God and brings about His judgment upon the land and the people who tolerate it.

Chapter Fourteen
Knowledge of the Law

1. The law must be published openly: Deuteronomy 27:1-4, 8.

2. The whole law must be read publicly at the end of every seventh or sabbatical year: Deuteronomy 31:9-13.

The number of laws given by God is a short one, 613 by the rabbinical reckoning which divides one law at times into several, less by Christian reckonings. It was mandatory that this body of laws be read and taught faithfully. In Joshua 8:30-32 we read that Joshua had the laws published in an open place; this assumes literacy on the part of the people. We see an instance of the public reading of the law in 2 Kings 23:1-3, an aspect of King Josiah's reformation.

The proverb, "Ignorance of the law is no excuse," has reference to Biblical law. Statist law, and especially bureaucratic law, requires great libraries to contain, so that ignorance of man's law is inescapable. *First*, the laws are too numerous for even lawyers to know; and, *second*, humanistic law has no basis in the order of things, whereas God's law is imprinted by the Creator in His creatures.

Where laws are too numerous for men to know, then knowledge of the law is restricted to specialists in the law, to lawyers. But humanistic law is too vast in volumes for even lawyers to know it all, so that specialization in particular fields becomes necessary. In the 1970s, the vice-president of an international bank said that the laws and regulations governing banking were so many and so contradictory that any banker could be imprisoned at the will of Federal authorities. This is now no doubt true of all of us.

It is questionable that a free society can long exist when its laws are unknown to most of the citizens. It is ironic that 20th century countries must emphasize education while at the same time keeping their peoples most ignorant of the law. This is a precondition of tyranny.

Today, who can know the law? Congress passes laws of more than 2,000 pages in length, which no member of Congress ever reads in full. This is a prescription for tyranny and dictatorship.

The Ten Commandments sum up God's law in ten sentences. All the laws which develop these Ten Commandments are comprehended in a short number of pages. They are *moral* premises which all men know, whether they accept them or not. Who can know the law of any state now? One lawyer has observed that the best and most learned men in criminal law are convicted criminals who spend their time in prison libraries studying the law to find loopholes in it. A society in which criminals know the law far better than the law-abiding citizenry is a strange one, to say the least.

Ignorance of God's law, a willful ignorance, is rampant in the churches, and by choice. For this ignorance, God will in some way exact His price.

3. The law must be studied: Deuteronomy 6:6-7, 20-25; 11:18-19. The requirement is that one teach them to the children and study them constantly, because God's law is the way of righteousness or justice for His redeemed peoples.

4. There can be no adding to or subtracting from God's law: Deuteronomy 4:1-2. The law is God's law, and man has no right to alter it, add to it, nor to subtract from it. It is God's grace that we are given His law as the way of life. Since we created neither ourselves nor this world, we must obey the Creator's law as His way of life for us. As Psalm 1 makes clear, those who do not delight in the law of the Lord have chosen death.

Chapter Fifteen
Damages

1. For a fire which damages property: Exodus 22:6. Restitution is required.

2. For injury to a neighbor: Leviticus 24:19. Restitution.

3. For stealing: Exodus 22:1-5; Leviticus 6:2-7. Here we have included in Leviticus 6:2-7, false swearing, breach of trust, and oppression of an neighbor.

4. For killing an animal belonging to another: Leviticus 24:18, 21.

5. For one animal killing another: Exodus 21:35-36.

6. For animals used as bailment, or borrowed, etc.: Exodus 22:10-12.

7. For animals that kill a person: Exodus 21:28-32, 35-36. Restitution. The animal shall be killed. If the animal has a record of being dangerous, and has not been kept penned, then the owner also must die.

8. If an animal falls into an uncovered pit, the owner of the pit must make restitution: Exodus 21:33-34.

9. For the loss of borrowed property: Exodus 22:14. Restitution.

10. A thief caught at once with the stolen animals in hand shall pay double restitution: Exodus 22:4.

11. An animal that escapes into another man's field and inflicts loss: the owner must make double restitution also.

12. Where a man is guilty of a breach of trust, he shall make a trespass offering at the sanctuary, restore in full the principal, and add 20 percent: Leviticus 6:1-5. This same penalty applies to wrongs committed against anyone; if the offended man be dead, and have no kin, "let the trespass be recompensed unto the LORD, even to the priest" (Num. 5:6-8). It is specified to the priest so that it becomes public; without this, there is no public awareness that the wrong has been righted.

It is clear from this how basic restitution and restoration are to God's law and will. The word *forgive* in modern languages has an *emotional* connotation, whereas Biblically it is *juridical*. It means normally that charges have been dropped because satisfaction has been rendered, but in the sentence from the Cross (Luke 23:34) it means "Defer the charges for the time being, for they know not what they do."

Chapter Sixteen
Law as Liberty

We have seen thus far that *restitution* is basic to God's law, its purpose being the *restoration* of godly order. This is a step towards the establishment of God's Kingdom, begun as men and women are made a new creation in Christ, and then furthered as they bring every area of life and thought into captivity to Christ.

The Western world, once known as Christendom, has abandoned its centuries old adherence to God's law for an antinomian and modernist position. (My father, a graduate of the University of Edinburgh and New Mound College prior to World War I, in his preaching echoed Edinburgh, but, in his day by day living, reflected his rural, old country adherence to the law-word of God.) This antinomianism has been an abandonment of the Faith, because whose law you follow, he is your god.

The horrifying premise of church thinking is that the law is bondage. That is indeed true *if you are a law-breaker*. The lawless man finds the law a fearful handicap. If priests and churchmen create and impose their own version of law upon us, it is a yoke and a hindrance.

But is this true of God's law, the law of the Holy One? James, the brother of our Lord, in James 1:25 and 2:12 (c.f. Gal. 5:1), speaks of "the perfect law of liberty," very obviously seeing the law as a blessing to the righteous.

Now the giver of law is the god of that society, whatever name he may be given. The law-giver defines good and evil, right and wrong, and he thereby ordains the course of that society; law is a key form of determination, and laws are given by rulers and states in order to set the course for a realm or social order. On the human scene, laws, together with social planning, regulations, and controls, are a humanistic form of predestination. We live in a time of fanatic dedication to humanistic, statist predestination, which, naturally, finds talk of predestination by God intolerable.

The choice for men is anarchy or law. But humanistic law is a form of anarchy because it has no relationship to God's fundamental order. Humanistic law thus leads to anarchy. By necessity, humanism has chosen the tempter's program, every man as his own god, knowing or deciding for himself what is good and evil (Gen. 3:5). In humanism, sometimes the individual is his own god; at other times, the state exercises this power for all the people.

Biblical faith means recognizing God's law as the ground of our freedom. *Law is liberty*, not slavery. If I am a murderer, the law is bondage and a yoke to me. If I am a godly man, it is freedom for me that law restrains the men who would like to see me dead. The law to me then is liberty from murderers, thieves, and others. How much freedom can any of us ever enjoy if we are suddenly in a world ruled by a Marquis de Sade, where all crimes are legal because they are *natural* (being the acts of fallen man), and only Christianity is illegal, because it is *supernatural* and hence anti-natural?

Law is liberty, and religious antinomianism is a guarantee of slavery because it exalts the laws of the fallen men over the law of God, and because it makes a holy cause of a contempt for God's law.

The psalmist asks, "Shall the throne of iniquity have fellowship with thee, which frameth mischief by a law?" (Ps. 94:20) In James McFatt's rendering, a paraphrase, this reads, "Can evil rulers have thee for our ally, who work us injury by law?"

Can there be a free society, the *professed* goal of modern men, when God's perfect law of liberty is despised? How free can any society be when it drops God's Ten Commandments, and the whole body of His law? It is no accident that the Western World, no longer Christendom, is moving into statist tyranny.

The cause of freedom is a futile one on anything other than God's terms, His Son the King, and His law our way of life. For men to seek freedom apart from God is comparable to seeking heaven in hell. The humanistic state constantly expands its power, because its goal, and the goal of its citizenry is to be as God, determining their own laws, lives, and morality (Gen. 3:5). Because it is not God, the humanistic state has a problem, never having enough power to play god as it hopes to do. As a result, by an ever expanding body of law, the humanistic state strives for the total power that is its dream.

Humanistic law means tyranny, whereas God's law is liberty. God's law cannot expand: it is a limited body of legislation, and, in much of the law, God reserves the right of judgment to Himself. Thus, little is left to man's discretion, if anything.

Humanistic law is a plan of salvation, a way to the good society as the humanist envisions it. God's law is not a plan of salvation but of sanctification, of holiness. The antinomians think that by denying God's law, they have preserved the integrity of Christian salvation when in fact they have denied it. *By embracing humanistic, statist law, they have adopted an anti-Christian plan of salvation.*

When Horace Mann promoted humanistic and statist education, together with civil government, as the means to heaven on earth, the Arminian churchmen of his day failed to see that, in adopting Mann's viewpoint, they were abandoning the premise of Christian faith, the sovereignty of God and salvation through Christ's statement and His Headship as our priest, prophet, and King. Horace Mann was quite openly a Unitarian, but too few were concerned about that. We are now surrounded by Mann's legacy, and too many treasure it because it is an old one, therefore good Americanism!

The culmination festival in the law is the jubilee which stresses liberty and release:

> And ye shall hallow the fiftieth year, and proclaim liberty throughout all the land unto all the inhabitants thereof: it shall be a jubilee unto you; and ye

shall return every man unto his possession, and ye shall return every man unto his family. (Lev. 25:10)

17. Ye shall not therefore oppress one another; but thou shalt fear thy God: for I am the Lord your God.
18. Wherefore ye shall do my statutes, and keep my judgments, and do them; and ye shall dwell in the land in safety.
19. And the land shall yield her fruit, and ye shall eat your fill, and dwell therein in safety. (Lev. 25:17-19)

God's law is full of promises of blessings to His people. Man's law is essentially punitive, not given ever to promising any good thing!

These questions need to be asked of all antinomians: What freedom can exist in a lawless society? And whose laws alone give justice and freedom? How we answer these questions will reveal who our God is.

Chapter Seventeen
Criminal Contempt for the Law

1. Defiance of and contempt for the law: Deuteronomy 17:12-13; Numbers 15:30-31. The death penalty is required for anyone who presumptuously breaks the law (Num. 15:31). The meaning is not that he has only broken a specific law, but *denied* the validity of God's law. Deuteronomy 17:12 tells us that he has rejected the admonition of the priest as well as of the judge. His offense is twofold: *first*, he has broken God's law, *second*, he has denied the validity of *God's* law, so that he has struck at the very foundation of society.

2. Perversion and obstruction of justice: Exodus 23:1-2, 6-7; Leviticus 19:15, 35-36. The crimes here include repeating baseless rumors, siding with evil men in court to give, in Moffatt's translation, "malicious evidence," tampering with justice to destroy a poor man, working to acquit evil men, and to condemn, even to death, innocent and guiltless people. Such perversions of justice include favoring the rich, or favoring the poor, rather than justice. Dishonesty in courts or in commerce works injustice. This makes mandatory justice in the courts and honesty in money and in commerce, honest measures and "hard" money, i.e., gold and/or silver.

3. Bribery is forbidden because it works to pervert justice: Exodus 23:8; Deuteronomy 16:19; 27:25. Bribery is spoken of as a kind of murder (Deut. 27:25), and, in all these texts, as a blinding of justice. It is also a perversion of justice. Partiality to one man or another must not take the place of honest testimony and honest verdicts.

4. Perjury: Deuteronomy 5:20; 19:16-20; Exodus 20:16; 23:1; Leviticus 19:12. The testimony of witnesses is the key aspect of court proceedings; without honest testimony there can be no justice. The moral failure of witnesses is basic to the failure of courts.

The penalty for perjury is the penalty for the crime of which is the concern of the court proceedings. If the potential penalty is death, the false witness must die.

One of the Ten Commandments is a condemnation of bearing false witness. The reference is essentially to a court of law; lying in general is secondary. A society without honest courts is soon a society without justice. Courts are all ultimately God's courts, whether they recognize Him or not. Justice is first of all God's concern because He is righteousness or justice. Where perjury prevails, injustice reigns.

Two of the Ten Commandments are concerned with speech. ("Thou shalt not take the Name of the LORD thy God in vain" has speech as a concern while having a broader reference, and "Thou shalt not bear a false witness" is also concerned with speech).

To cheapen language is to cheapen life. Character and integrity are basic to a godly man, and godly society. The cheapening and the vulgarization of language are devastating to life and community. In decaying Rome, as in the decaying world of the 20th century, language becomes less a means of communication and community and more and more a weapon to cheapen and degrade men and morals.

Perjury is a criminal contempt for the law and for God and man. The inclusion of perjury in the list of offenses cited for cursing on Mount Ebal (Deut. 27:25) is important because the list is of sins which radically destroy society. All sin is destructive of and is a war against community, and perjury is emphatically such an offense.

Deuteronomy 17:12 is especially important because it cites disobedience to the pastoral warning against perjury. How serious it is then when pastors do not teach this and other laws of God? They share as a result the guilt that is the lot of an accursed society. In Deuteronomy 27 we see that sins mark such an accursed society.

Chapter Eighteen
Punishment

1. Restitution: Exodus 22:1ff. Depending on the value of whatever is stolen, destroyed, or damaged, restitution could be from death to fivefold. Thus, because oxen were beasts of burden and required much training, and their meat and hide had value, their restitution was fivefold; sheep, whose wool and meat had value, as do their reproductive capacity, required fourfold restitution. Restitution began with a restoration of what was stolen plus an equivalent amount.

2. In certain offenses, it was restoration plus 20 percent: this applies to cases where something rightly belonging to God was retained or used by someone in ignorance (Lev. 5:16). This also applied to cases where someone took advantage of a neighbor, restoration plus 20 percent (Lev. 6:1-7; Num. 5:7).

3. The law could not be taken into one's own hands: Leviticus 19:18. We are not God; we have a duty to God to obey His law and to love our neighbor, which means keeping the law in all our dealings with Him, because love does not wrong a neighbor but observes God's law in dealing with him, for love is the fulfillment, i.e., the putting into force of the law (Rom. 13:10).

4. In minor offenses, not requiring restitution, where some kind of punishment is deemed necessary, corporal punishment is required: Deuteronomy 25:1-3. If it be a beating or a whipping, no more than 40 stripes can be given. The offender is not to be degraded but simply chastised. This law was on the books in many American states well into this century and, earlier, commonly applied.

5. Imprisonment: Leviticus 24:12; Numbers 15:34. Imprisonment was temporary, pending a trial. It was not a means of punishment. After trial, it could be death, restitution, or corporal punishment.

6. The extent of punishment: Leviticus 19:18; Deuteronomy 24:16. Everyone shall be punished for his own sins; the fathers cannot be punished for their children's sins, nor children for their father's. If there is complicity in a family member's sin, then there is guilt, but not otherwise.

7. No ransom or fine is permitted in cases or murder: Numbers 35:30-31. The death penalty is mandatory in murder cases. In Exodus 21:28, where we have an ox fatally killing someone, in cases other than these where the owner's ox has been known to be vicious, and therefore both ox and owner must be put to death (Ex. 21:29), a ransom or restitution can be the sentence of the court upon the owner (Ex. 21:30).

8. Other forms of punishment: Leviticus 20:14 and 21:9 prescribe burning. This may have been a cremation after execution. In Leviticus 21:9, it is for a priest's daughter who becomes a prostitute and thereby strikes at her father's

office, and in Leviticus 20:14 this death penalty applies to a case where a man commits incest with a wife and her mother: all three are to die. They are to be burned because even their bodies pollute the land. In Deuteronomy 25:11-12, a woman who, when her husband is fighting with another man, seizes the other man's genitals to incapacitate him, is to have her hand cut off without compassion. These are unusual cases and are intended to stress the evilness of the offense. In Deuteronomy 21:22-23, we are told that hanged men cannot remain hanging more than one day.

9. *Lex talionis*: Exodus 21:24-25; Deuteronomy 19:21; Leviticus 24:19-20; Numbers 35:33. The eye for an eye, tooth for a tooth, hand for a hand, foot for a foot formula means that the punishment must fit the crime. The penalties for specific offenses are routinely given. The *lex talionis* statements do not stipulate another kind of penalty but simply sum up the premise of the law that, insofar as possible, restitution must be made, or a comparable fine or penalty assessed. From the time of the Greeks to the present, misreadings of the Bible have been prevalent. The perspective of Greek philosophy predisposed men to reduce everything to abstractions and often to read particular statements in their crudest sense. God is the ultimate Person and power: He is not an abstraction but the Supreme Being and totally personal. His revelation is therefore particular and personal, not abstract. For the Aristotelian and Platonic mind, the Bible is a crude book. For the Biblically governed mind, the Greek philosophers are airy bubbleheads living in the clouds of their foolish minds. Each to the other appears ridiculous, but the important question is not one of appearance but of truth. If the God of the Bible is denied, there is nothing.

Biblical law tells us that there are consequences to all human action, in time and in eternity. Because there is an ultimate right and wrong, good and evil, there is a heaven and a hell. The deterioration of justice in this world follows a denial of justice in the world to come. When man denies the validity of good and evil *and* the necessity for and the consequences of decisions, then he denies the reality of a future. The future is the consequence of the present. The goal of a static world, the behavior or ant-hill goal of Marxists, socialists, and statists, is a futureless world. The views of such a world envision no religion, no morality, no marriage, and no meaning except "the acceptance of self as God."[1] To deny God's law is to replace it with man's law, the goal of which is to replace God's justice with man's changing, statist whims of tyranny. The purpose of God's law is our freedom under God whereas the purpose of humanistic statist laws is freedom from God but slavery to the state.

The insistence of humanism, as in the *Humanist Manifesto I and II*, is freedom from God. But freedom from God is freedom from life and freedom. It is freedom for death to reign.

[1.] Peter Loril and Sidd Murray-Clark, *History of the Future* (New York, N.Y. Doubleday, 1989.), p. 57.

To deny the validity of God's law is far worse than denying the validity of medicine and surgery where needed. The society which departs from God's law leaves behind health, healing, and freedom for a license to sin and die.

10. Brutality to a bondservant or slave: Exodus 21:26. If a man, angry at a servant, struck a male or female servant in such a way that an eye, or a tooth, were destroyed, or comparable damage done, then the servant went free. If a foreigner, their slavery ended; if an Israelite bondservant, the rest of their service was cancelled.

11. The case of death by a goring ox: Exodus 21:28-32. If the goring ox were not previously known to be dangerous, there was no guilt on the part of the owner: it was an accident. If the ox had a record of being dangerous, both the ox and the owner were to be killed. If the ox injures someone's servants, the compensation to the servants' master must be 30 shekels of silver for each offense.

12. If a thief invades a house at night, he can be killed without liability, but if he be killed without provocation in a daytime break-in, that is manslaughter. The thief must make full restitution, he shall be sold as a bondservant to make restitution. The restitution is to be at least double (Exodus 22:1-4).

13. Borrowed property: Exodus 22:9-15. If any borrowed animal should die without known cause, or be taken or driven away without the borrower's complicity, on an oath, the borrower is declared innocent. Otherwise, double restitution follows. If negligence has led to theft, then restitution is required, otherwise not.

If hired property is injured or broken, and the owner is there as a part of the hire, there is no liability. If a wild animal has killed the borrowed animal, there is no liability.

14. Arson: Exodus 22:6. The penalty is restitution, whether the arson is accidental or malicious.

15. Killing a farm animal: Leviticus 24:18, 21. Restitution is required, "beast for beast."

16. Removing landmarks: Deuteronomy 19:14; 27:17; Proverbs 23:10. Changing the location of landmarks was a form of stealing land. No penalty is cited, but it invokes God's strong condemnation and curse.

17. Hazardous pits: Exodus 21:33-34. To leave an open pit wherein stray animals can fall is wrong; the owner of the pit shall pay for the dead animal, which then becomes his property for whatever value the hide can bring.

18. Fighting animals: Exodus 21:35-36. If two animals fight, and one kills the other, the survivor shall be sold, and the proceeds shared for the equivalent amount paid to the owner of the dead animal. If the killer ox had been known to be dangerous, and the owner had not kept him in, the owner of the aggressive ox shall pay the owner for the dead ox, and take possession of it.

19. Criminal trespass: Exodus 22:5. Animal trespass could be accidental (a form of animal getting loose and entering another man's vineyard or field), or deliberate (turned into the field to get free food), restitution is mandatory.

It should be apparent by now that in most offenses restitution is the usual and normal penalty, from double to fivefold usually. With restitution, crime does not pay. The penalty is too great to risk.

Since no prison system for punishment is a part of Biblical law, this means that all serious crimes lead either to the execution of the offender, or to restitution. This helps prevent the rise of a class of habitual criminals whose livelihood is crime. What God's law presupposes is that, where obeyed, only the people whose offenses are the results of weakness rather than perversity are likely to survive.

Chapter Nineteen
Property

The Biblical doctrine of property is very important for us to understand because it is so basic to the knowledge of Biblical faith. Neither man and especially the state is the owner of this earth: God alone is. "The earth is the LORD'S, and the fullness thereof; the world, and they that dwell therein" (Ps. 24:1). Not only the world but we, the people, are God's property. We are called His sheep (Ps. 95:7; 100:3, etc.), not a complimentary term. Sheep have no rights as against owners. He is God the Lord, the Creator, and we are the sheep of His pasture.

This means that the state has neither title to property nor *legitimate* power to tax it. We are taxed because of our sins; we have made the state our god and our shepherd. Men prefer the state's tax to God's tithe; the state takes far more of our wealth than does God, but God requires moral responsibility of us. We prefer rather to be taxed and to whine than to tithe and be godly men.

The state of property is thus indicative of the moral and religious condition of a people. People are very prone to blame the state for their own moral dereliction.

Property is a test of character. If we are stewards unto God and accountable to Him for our use of wealth, of land, and of His various gifts, we cannot assume that our own ultimacy can be a legitimate position. We are God's property: we are not our own.

Land is in Biblical law that form of property most clearly governed by God's law. The buying and selling of other forms of property was routine. Land was allotted to the tribes (Num. 26:52-56), and given to their families (Num. 33:54). The clans could not exchange lands (Num. 36:2; Joshua 18:2-10). After a disaster, such as the exile, there was a re-allotment (Ezekiel 45:1-8; 46:16-18; 47). The Levites received cities and suburbs, lands which could be resold. They had as individuals no inheritance (Num. 35:2-5; Deut. 18:1-2; Joshua 21:3-42). Their service was to be in all the tribes. In ordinary times, the land could not be sold in perpetuity but only leased (Lev. 25:23-34; 25:13-16; 27:16-20). The jubilee was the 50th year, when the rural lands reverted to the original owners. The Levites could redeem their urban lands then but not other urban dwellers (Lev. 25:30-33); in fact, the Levites could redeem their property at any time by repayment (Lev. 25:32).

The Ten Commandments say clearly, "Thou shalt not steal" (Ex. 20:15; Deut. 5:19). Property thus is not a capitalistic invention but the ordination of God. Property is an instrument and test of responsibility and a test of man's character. It is instrumental in the exercise of dominion. Every unjust social order works to control and/or confiscate property, for the control of property becomes the control of man.

Capitalism has come to mean the separation of property from God and His law, and this development has led to the decay of capitalism. By undermining the Biblical doctrine of property, capitalism has undermined itself. The godless state and the godless corporation are alike in their disregard for the theological meaning of property.

Man, together with his family and possessions, is God's property, and to be used for His service and glory. If property is separated from God, it is then given to man or to the state. Man, the male, as property owner, has been able in history to prostitute his daughters, his wife, or his sons as their master. The state has used man in a variety of ways as canon fodder, a cow to be milked financially, and so on. Only as God's property can people escape enslavement.

We must remember that the allotment of land was to *families*, not to isolated, anarchistic individuals.

Property is the means whereby godly dominion can be exercised. If we deny to Christian man the mandate to exercise dominion over the earth, we then give to sinful man and the pagan state the power to exercise dominion. For the Christian, it means *work*, for the anti-Christian, it means *theft*, the supposed right to expropriate from others in the name of the common good.

Because property is a form of power, ungodly men resent any control of property other than their own. As the self-elected elite philosopher-kings, they believe that the world must be governed by their wisdom rather than God's word.

God does not share His glory nor law-making power with others, so that all attempts by man or the state to become the basic owners of property are an affront to God. Many men are quick to see statist usurpations of the control of property but are less willing to see their own transgressions against God. Men have been no less eager to replace God than the state, if not more so.

In cases of sales of personal property to one's neighbor, the general rule was to avoid defrauding one's neighbor (Lev. 25:14).

Where loans were involved, no man could take a hand mill or the upper millstone as security for a loan, because this involved taking life in pledge, i.e., the means of survival (Deut. 24:6). If a coat were taken as security, it could not be kept overnight because the poor slept with the coat as their covering (Ex. 22:26-27; Deut. 24:12-13). The creditor must not enter a poor man's house to choose the pledge; this shames and degrades him. He must wait for the man to bring an acceptable pledge to him (Deut. 24:10-11).

Chapter Twenty
Usury or Interest

The word *usury* has gained a meaning that falsifies the picture so that for many it means exorbitant interest. The subject of interest is colored by the Greek view of it as evil.

In Biblical law, interest is forbidden to anyone lending to a fellow believer who is in need. We must not see ourselves then as a creditor but as a friend, and the loan is to be interest-free (Ex. 22:25; Deut. 23:19-20). Interest can be charged on a loan to an alien, one who is not a covenant member (Deut. 23:20). A covenant member, a brother, when in need, should receive a loan without interest (Deut. 15:7-8).

Debts to aliens who are not covenant members are not cancelled on the seventh or sabbatical years (Deut. 15:1-6).

From Abraham's day on, Israel or the Hebrew people were a mixed multitude of various peoples. Their common tie was the covenant, not blood. As a result, we cannot limit the exemption from interest in charitable loans to Israelites alone for to do so is to disregard the covenant. To view *Israel* as a racial group is to impose modern ideas on the Bible. Neither nationalism nor race were then governing factors. A covenant constituted a group, clan or tribe, or a people. Roman citizenship centuries after Moses rested on "worship" and the rites of lustration or atonement. The basic bond that constituted a people was religious, not necessarily or usually a true faith, but a faith nonetheless.

Chapter Twenty-One
Creditors and Debtors

The realm of money and debts was not a morally neutral realm in God's law but a sphere of moral responsibility. Neither creditor nor debtor lives in an area of freedom from law and ethics but always under God.

One distinction, however, was notable. God's redeemed people are a free people in the crucial area: they are delivered from the power and penalty of sin. They have therefore the ability to use freedom. God's law permits the ungodly to contract long-term debts. The world of the 1990s is dedicated to long-term debt as a way of life, and God permits it, knowing that it is a way of death.

For the godly, debts must be limited to six years (Deut. 15:1-6, 12-18). We are God's people, and we must not be man's slave, for debt is the world's most popular form of slavery. Debt then led often to bond-service to work off a debt. Such persons were not to be treated as slaves but as a hired hand or temporary resident until repayment or the jubilee (Lev. 25:39-42).

The covenant people were to be a *free* people, and therefore their ability to contract long-term debt was denied. This ability to contract long-term debt is a license to slavery, for slavery is ownership in another man's labor. Too many people pay up to 50 percent of their income to creditors, and this is surely a form of servitude. With World War II, and the rise of modernism and antinomianism, bank loans in the United States went from five year notes to twenty and thirty year mortgages. This was seen by most as a benefit rather than as slavery.

As a general rule, God requires that we "owe no man anything, but to love one another" (Rom. 13:8). In cases of troubles and needs, short-term debt is permitted, up to six years. Now the prevailing opinion is that long-term debt is good both for men and nations. We shall pay a price for such a belief.

Chapter Twenty-Two
The Law as Death

For the godly, God's law is liberty. It protects man from the lawless actions of thieves and murderers, for example. If, however, a man be a criminal, the law is at the least a restriction on his freedom, and it is potentially his death.

What we think of God's law tells us what we are. For example, Leviticus 20:10 requires death for adultery, the death of both the adulterer and the adulteress. Leviticus 20:13 requires death for homosexual acts. Over the years, many have demanded, "Do you believe in that?" Well, God said it, and I accept it as His requirement of a good society. All too many people, unbelievers and churchmen alike, seethe with hostility against God for so ruling, and against me for so believing in God's law. Why? Do they want these and like sins to be an option for them if they so choose? Do they want all immoral and moral life "styles" to be equally valid? Or do they only want God as a spectator and inspirer but never as lawmaker and judge?

Law is liberty to the godly. It protects them from evil-doers, from criminals. Their lives and possessions are secure where God's law is honored, jeopardized where God's law is despised.

For the ungodly, God's law is a sentence of death, in time and in eternity. Separation from God, and from His law which is the expression of His nature, is death. All through Scripture, God's nature is described as altogether *righteous*, meaning altogether *justice*. The law of God sets forth His justice or righteousness. It is only natural for the ungodly to hate God's law. Whatever their profession, they see God's law as a death sentence against them.

How we think of God's law tells us how we think of God. If we go through the Bible to eliminate or re-interpret those aspects of God displeasing to us, we have eliminated the living God to create a false god, an idol, out of some of God's words and attributes. Idolatry does not necessarily require materials to create a false image; we can create idols with our ideas, or with selected texts from the Bible.

For us, the law of God can be liberty, or it can be death.

Chapter Twenty-Three
Crimes Against the Family

1. Adultery: Exodus 20:14; Deuteronomy 5:18; 22:22-24; Leviticus 18:20; 20:10. No advanced culture has long existed once adultery is tolerated because it is destructive of family life and of personal and social stability. God's law legislates against adultery on the part of both men and women. No man lives unto himself, and his sexual activity has social consequences of a far-reaching kind. Because the family is God's basic governmental institution for men, His law surrounds the family with protective legislation. Adultery is treason against the family, God's essential governing body.

2. The penalty: Deuteronomy 22:20-29; Leviticus 20:10. At one time, treason was against the church, in most of history, against the state. At present, with the breakdown of the state, treason is poorly defined. In a godly society, treason is against the family. The penalty is death. In any society, the law of treason protects whatever is most important to that society. Where *persons* are concerned, the law against murder protects them. With the family, it is the death penalty for adultery. It is curious that a number of churches are hostile to divorce but less harsh against adultery. In Biblical law, death for adultery is a form of divorce, i.e., by execution. In the 20th century especially, the family is less respected by the law, and adultery, however regarded by the church, is a private option.

3. Rape: Deuteronomy 22:25-29. The penalty for rape is death. If it be seduction (Ex. 22:16-17), a man must pay her "the dowry of virgins," a considerable sum. If he offers to marry the girl, acceptance or rejection rests with the father. In either case, the payment of a dowry was mandatory. As a result, seduction and rape, because of their severe penalties, were not appealing options.

At this point, many will hold that these laws worked once in a more rural society; it is held that in our present great population centers, such laws would never function. However, in great urban centers today we have communities, sometimes both religious and national, where *the controls on all are very real because nobody is anonymous.* When social institutions other than the state weaken, anonymity sets in, and also lawlessness. Where people are anonymous, crime increases. The modern world is saturated with anonymity because the modern state has undermined all rival powers. The lust for anonymity with some people is a desire to be free to sin without recognition. The growth of the modern city came when transportation had advanced so that goods could be shipped from almost anywhere in the country, but people flocked to the cities because they wanted anonymity. Anonymity or darkness is appealing to many sinners.

Sexual crimes are very serious in God's sight because the family is ordained by Him to be the central institution in man's life, more important than state or church, and holding the basic powers that govern the future: children, property, inheritance, education, and charity, all now being usurped by the state, because the state wants to govern both the present and the future.

By giving so central an emphasis to family law, God makes clear how important the family should be to us *because it is so very important to Him.* True, there is neither marrying, nor giving in marriage in heaven (Matt. 22:29-30), but neither is there preaching, medical care, elections, and more. Should we therefore abandon these things here? If something is important enough for God to include it in His word, it had better be very important to us.

4. Prostitution: Leviticus 19:29; 21:9; Deuteronomy 23:17-18. God prohibits prostitution, but only in one instance is it punished; when the daughter of a priest becomes a prostitute she profanes her father and is to be executed: it is an offense against both God and her father because of his office.

5. Incest: Leviticus 18:6-18; Deuteronomy 22:30; 27:20, 22-23. Because this especially is a secret sin, not easily exposed nor witnesses available, no penalty is cited except the curse of God, of a very total kind.

6. Seduction: Exodus 22:16-17; Deuteronomy 22:28-29. The Exodus text cites cases of seduction, where, if the man is acceptable to the girl's father, marriage can be required by him; in any case he must pay the dowry of a virgin. The law of Deuteronomy 22:28-29 deals with an instance when the seduction or rape took place where her cries could not be heard, and it is difficult to determine whether or not it is seduction or rape, then he shall pay a dowry and marry her with no right to divorce her.

6. Sexual acts during menstruation: Leviticus 18:19; 20:18. The penalty is excommunication.

7. Transvestite behavior: Deuteronomy 22:5. This is strongly forbidden but not punishable by man. It is an abomination to God. In a godly society, such conduct will be its own punishment.

8. Sexual assault: Deuteronomy 25:11-12. No woman can defend her husband in a fight by attacking his assailant's "private parts." This offense is so seriously regarded that the penalty is cutting off her hand. The implications here are far-reaching. If men in wartime attack civilians, mothers, women generally, and children, should not their penalty be similarly severe?

9. Bestiality: Exodus 22:19; Leviticus 18:23; 20:15-16; Deuteronomy 27:21. The penalty is death, both for the man or woman, and for the animal. In one major city at least, animals for such sexual use are openly advertised. Such acts are an open defiance of God's order, and, here as elsewhere, the pleasure is in the perversity of the act.

10. Sodomy, or homosexuality: Leviticus 18:22; 20:13; Deuteronomy 23:17f.; Romans 1:24-32. In Romans 1:27, this is called the burning out, or, the flaming out of man, the ultimate form of rebellion against God and His law order. As a result, the penalty is unequivocally death. Romans implies (1:32) that the penalty applies to both sexes.

In Leviticus 18:5, the sexual laws are prefaced with the statement: "Ye shall therefore keep my statutes, and my judgments, which if a man do, he shall live in them: I am the LORD." This ties in with the commandment, "Honour thy father and thy mother: that thy days may be long upon the land which the LORD thy God giveth thee" (Ex. 20:12). *Life* is promised thus for both the physical and spiritual faithfulness to the family. Crimes against the family are crimes against God. If the penalty to a society be as severe as God declares it to be, should we be surprised that it is severe against individuals? Without persons, there is no church, nor state, nor society. God speaks first to us as persons. Without us, nothing else can exist.

It would appear from the foregoing that no penalties are attached to prostitution except in the case of a priest's daughter (Lev. 21:9); to assume this would be an error. Prostitution does not take place outside the context of life and relationships. The man who goes into a prostitute, and sometimes the prostitute as well, is commonly married. This has a penalty, death (Lev. 20:10; Deut. 22:22-25). Simply because it is for hire does not make an act of prostitution any the less adulterous.

Chapter Twenty-Four
Murder and Manslaughter

One of the Ten Commandments forbids murder (Ex. 20:13; Deut. 5:17). The requirement of death appears as early as Noah's day (Gen. 9:6), although it is clear that Cain recognized the death penalty (Gen. 4:14). The reason for this penalty is given in Genesis 9:6, "Whoso sheddeth man's blood, by man shall his blood be shed: for in the image of God made he man." However depraved and evil the man, his life cannot be taken except by due process of law, in wartime in self-defense, and in defending one's home at night from a thief who has broken in (Ex. 22:2). God who created man and his life totally governs the taking of life.

1. "Thou shalt not kill:" Exodus 20:12; Deuteronomy 5:17; 19:11-13; Genesis 9:5-6; Exodus 21:12, 14; 20:12; Leviticus 24:17, 21; Numbers 35:15, 33. In Exodus 21:15 the death penalty for patricide or matricide is strongly stressed. Sacrificing a child to Molech requires the death penalty (Lev. 20:2-5).

2. Manslaughter, or accidental death, did not qualify for the death penalty, and cities of refuge were provided as a refuge for the man from avenging kinsmen (Num. 35:10ff.).

3. As noted above, self-defense is not murder if it involves killing a criminal (Ex. 22:2).

4. A farm or household animal that kills a person must be killed: Exodus 21:28-32. Persons who keep an animal with a record of attacking people must die if the animal with a known history of injury to persons is guilty of killing someone. The owner is also guilty and must die.

5. Habitual criminals must die on conviction: Deuteronomy 21:18-21. This law has a long history in American law. What is unusual about its Biblical statement is the part of the criminal's parents, if alive. They must stand with God's law against their son; truth must prevail over blood. God's requirement takes precedence over family ties.

6. Death by miscarriage: Exodus 21:22-25. If men in fighting hurt a nearby pregnant woman, so that a miscarriage follows, then the husband can impose a monetary penalty, if the judges agree; but if death ensues for the aborted child, this penalty is death. If this be true of accidental abortion, how much more so of a willful one? This is an important issue since c. 1970, and an emotional one. We cannot be governed by our emotions, but only by God's law. Some years ago, in shock over two horrifying cases of rape, incest, and pregnancy, that came tardily to my attention, I wrote a paragraph excepting some such cases from bans on abortion, a very serious error on my part. We are told in Isaiah 8:20, "To the law and to the testimony: if they speak not according to this word, it is because there is no light in them." Since then, I have tried to speak according to the light of God's word.

7. Stealing and selling a man: Exodus 21:16; Deuteronomy 24:7. Enslaving people is punishable by death. The qualification here is that the person be a covenant member. However, this was no license to enslave foreigners. Aliens, non-covenant peoples, were readily and freely marketed everywhere in antiquity, and it was permissible for Hebrews to buy and own them. However, if the slave converted he could go free. His treatment, in any case, had to be godly; if treated badly, and taking flight, he could not be caught and returned (Deut. 23:15-16). Southern defenders of slavery on "Biblical" grounds did not do justice to such texts, and fugitive slaves were hunted ruthlessly. Any slave who was maimed, whether Hebrew or not, went free (Ex. 21:26-27). The slave was to be circumcised to be made a member of the covenant (Ex. 12:44). The Bible recognized slavery to sin as a part of fallen man's condition, and this slavery to sin leads to other forms of enslavement, but the goal is freedom in Christ.

8. The false prophet: Deuteronomy 13:1-4; 17:2-5. The penalty is death for any advocate of a false faith who rises up "in the midst of thee," and who seeks to supplant the faith. No penalty is prescribed for pagans in the land, only for those who try to subvert the faith, which is treason. This penalty has a bad history because of its use against dissidents from the *church* rather than the triune God. The church is not Christ, and, when Scripture speaks of it, it is as *the body* of Christ's new humanity, not His deity. Too often the church claims continuity with Christ's deity, which is blasphemy.

9. Presumptuous defiance of the court: Deuteronomy 13:6-18; 17:12; Leviticus 24:15-16. Both priest and judge sat in courts to render judgment. Any man who refused to obey the law and expressed defiant contempt for it was to die after trial. To deny the foundation of the law can be worse than breaking it at some point. Blasphemy can involve this same offense. The essence of such an apostasy is a revolution against the law order: it is a summons to revolution. All revolutions are at heart religious in their goals.

The first line of defense for human life is religious. Different religions have differing ideas about human life, from a contempt of it to a misplaced veneration of it. The Biblical perspective is that man's life has value, not because of man nor what he is, but because man's image reflects God, and God protects His image bearer. We can take a man's life on God's terms, not our own.

Murder is now defined humanistically because man is defined after Darwin. We cannot have the same respect for man if he is no more than a higher ape. At present, many insist, curiously, in view of their evolutionary faith, on opposing capital punishment for murder although, in their perspective, life is a long and bloody struggle for survival. To prize life over justice is a view that in time can forfeit life together with justice. Of course, without God, justice itself erodes into nothing. The murder of law and of godly society is a major activity of the 20th century.

Chapter Twenty-Five
Lawless Alliances

> No alliances permitted with foreign nations who do not share in the covenant and the covenant faith: Exodus 34:12-16; Exodus 23:31-33; Deuteronomy 7:1-6.

It is impossible to understand this law unless we recognize that treaties, covenants, and marriages are *legal* arrangements. Every religion has its own system of laws, and, in various cultures, many evils have been legal: the sutee or burning of widows, human sacrifices, ritual prostitution, bestiality, homosexuality, murder of aliens, and so on. Religion has as its expression an ethical code and a system of laws. Law and morality differ from religion to religion. Marriage, for example, has a different meaning to a Christian, a Hindu, a Muslim, and a Buddhist. Differing moralities are all in some sense and at many points warring moralities. If two persons of differing religions marry, there will be either conflict or surrender.

All such unions, personal (i.e., marital), or by international treaty, are thus forbidden. In the 20th century, some nations have actually seen words and meanings simply as potential investments of war, ways of deluding and overcoming others.

For this reason, no religious intermarriages are permitted, nor treaties with nations with ungodly faiths. This is one side of this law: no covenanting of any kind either on the personal or the national side with the ungodly. Another aspect of this law assumes the likelihood of conflict. Then there is a requirement, when the enemy is defeated in the event of war, to destroy the temples and images of their false religion. This carries the war against their false religion rather than their persons.

Because every law system is an expression of a religious faith, we cannot view other law orders as comparable to ours. Laws can embody evil as well as good. The fact that something is called *law* does not make it *good*. Over the centuries to the present, much evil has been made into law. When man makes law, law will reflect his evil. We therefore must look to God for just laws.

The goal of the 20th century has been the rule of international law, a radically humanistic concept which requires the death of all other legal systems, most prominently the Biblical. To seek such a law, i.e., international, humanistic law, is to violate the fundamental commandment, "Thou shalt have no other gods before me" (Ex. 20:3). All alliances which set aside Biblical premises are unholy alliances, and they incur the judgment of God.

God's law here is clear, and yet, by and large, the churches have been silent concerning it, one of the sad facts of our time and an invitation to judgment (1 Peter 4:17).

There is no penalty here except the judgment of God.

Chapter Twenty-Six
The Source of Law

When God begins the Ten Commandments with the words, "Thou shalt have no other gods before me" (Ex. 20:3; Deut. 5:7), He not only bans the worship of any other gods but also the acceptance of any other laws than His own. Because He is the Lord who delivered His people "out of the house of bondage" (Ex. 20:2), out of slavery, He especially has the doubly legitimate claim on them to obey His law. He is, *first*, their Creator, and, *second*, their Redeemer: hence obedience to His law is mandatory.

In any system of thought the effectual god of that system is the source of law. He is the Definer. In any culture, the Definer determines and identifies the meaning of things and their qualities; whatever is, can only be known in terms of the defining factor. In the Bible, God is the Creator, Determiner, and the Definer. In Genesis 2, Adam is given the task of naming the animals, i.e., classifying them, for to *name* means to define and classify. This is to be done under God, in terms of His creating purposes. The *naming* meant to understand God's creative order.

Now, without Biblical faith, both man and the state will play god. This is original sin (Gen. 3:5). *God* is a necessary concept in human thought because some kind of ultimacy must exist, if not God, then man.

For example, Randell Craig Fasnacht, Jr., in *Life Child: The End of Poverty, The Case for Licensing all Parents*[1], gives us a Darwinian faith. He presupposes the necessary total control of man by a world state to eliminate poverty, retardation, disease, and death. All youth must complete two years of national service. All couples are limited to two children; all births must be licensed. Prior to conception, all couples must have lived together for three years, whether married or not. World poverty, death, war, hunger, nuclear weapons and more must be eliminated. This movement "points that man is God."[2] Virtually no freedom is allowed to individuals, but they are to think of themselves as God!

Cash will be eliminated. There will be a search for intelligent life in other solar systems, with the assurance "that those civilizations are at least 1 million years older than ours."[3] A major good "...is the elimination of death — within 50 years we could have the capability to live forever, with healthy bodies and minds."[4] This would mean 2042 at the latest.

There will be population control. A computerized and full history for every citizen will be compiled and will be available to anyone. And so on and so on.

---

[1] R. C. Fasnacht, Jr., *Life Child: The End of Poverty, The Case for Licensing all Parents*, Albany, N.Y.: Lifeforce Institute; 1992.
[2] *ibid.*, p. 2.
[3] *ibid.*, p. 65.
[4] *ibid.*, p. 59.

Given the premise that man is God, this is a logical perspective. But, since man is not God, the logical alternative is that God is God, and His law must bind us. For the churches to be antinomian is to shift the source of law from God to man. Having done so, it is illogical for them to quibble when the state legalizes abortion, homosexuality, or anything else. They have already transferred the law-making, defining, and determining powers from God to man and the state.

The hostility to theonomy and Christian reconstruction rests in the recognition that such a faith refuses to surrender God's claims on man and the state. Fasnacht, having defined God, quite logically transfers law-making, defining, and predestination to the state. Too much of the thinking within the church is illogical; it represents a syncretistic approach, a combination of those elements in Christianity and humanism most congenial to the religious dilettante. Such a perspective has proven to be an avenue to both success and impotence.

If our source of law is not God, we shall have tyranny in the name of sweetness and light.

In the summer of 1996, the Spartanburg, South Carolina County Council, disturbed by the growing endorsement of homosexuality by officials of public education, passed a resolution condemning such stances and affirming "the standards to which this community subscribes." A great outcry resulted, led by pro-homosexuals and by the media. The Greenville County Clergy issued a statement which said in part,

> We believe that sexuality is a deeply personal matter about which reasonable and godly people have vastly differing opinions. We feel that this is properly a matter between a people and their God.
>
> We believe that the real "standards of our community" are honesty, integrity, cooperation, respect for the law, and willingness to contribute time and energy to the life of the community. Good citizenship knows no bounds of religion, skin, color, ethnicity — or "sexual lifestyle."[5]

Such statements by the clergy are now routine. Respect for what law did these clergymen of Greenville County call for, God's or man's? Obviously God's law was in no way considered a valid standard.

Of course, the business community very early surrendered to the pressure by the pro-homosexuals. Amoral capitalism is the ever-increasing ally of anti-Christianity because a moral stance is intolerable where profits are involved. Modern-day capitalism often does not believe in a free market, preferring a controlled one. Being capitalistic no more insures goodness than does being a church member.

The spirit of Pilate marks much of history. When Pilate said, "What is truth?" (John 18:38), he was not asking a question but rather dismissing the subject as

---

[5.] Tom Landress, "The Politics of the Torch," in the *Southern Partisan*, 2nd Quarter, 1996, p. 25.

unrealistic, impractical or utopian. Pragmatism marks their perspective. But, as St.Paul warns us, "Be not deceived; God is not mocked: for whatsoever a man soweth, that shall he also reap" (Gal. 6:7).

Chapter Twenty-Seven
Insane Thinking About the Law

I frequently get telephone calls and letters, attacking me for affirming Biblical law. The questions begin thus: "Do you believe that homosexuals should be executed?" My answer always is simply that God so requires it in the Bible, and, as an interpreter of and a believer in the Bible, I do not believe that I have the right to disagree with God. The next question is usually this: how then can you be a Christian since Jesus said, "He that is without sin among you, let him first cast a stone" (John 8:7)? I try to explain that, *first*, an ancient premise of law requires that those who take part in a trial have "clean hands" in the matter, i.e., no thief can take part in a trial for theft as a credible witness. *Second*, if no man can be a part of a trial unless he is sinless, then, since we are all sinners, there can be no law, no courts, no police, no penalty, for crime since we all are sinners. This does not seem to disconcert most questioners.

This means that contemporary antinomianism is moving logically and steadily into the thinking of the Marquis de Sade. Sade held that any act committed was a natural and therefore a good act. Theft, murder, rape, incest, sodomy, and all the sins condemned by God, being *natural* were therefore *good*. Only Christianity and its faith and law were evil because they were supernatural.

It is interesting that the first question is usually about homosexuality. In personal confrontations, such questioners commonly refuse to answer the question, "Are *you* a homosexual, or, Why are homosexuals such a key concern for you?" Homosexuality has become a central intellectual concern because it is a central offense against God, and the essential *burning out* of man in his hatred of and war against God. (In Romans 1:27 "burned" should be translated as "burned out.") Questions about God's law on homosexuality are ways of challenging God's moral status! Some questioners insist that Jesus demanded the death of the law, despite His statement in Matthew 5:17-19. Such opinions reflect William Blake and ancient and modern gnosticism.

Another statement common to such critics is that to affirm God's law is to affirm hate! But hatred of what? To affirm God's law means that one wants to protect people from rape, murder, theft, and lawlessness in all its aspects. In the post-World War II years, I have unhappily known of many, many cases of rape, some of particularly vicious and sadistic character. Whom do these antinomians propose to love, the rapists or the victims? Some will insist on demanding that we "hate the sin and love the sinner." But sin does not exist in the abstract; it is an act of men and an expression of their nature. Some rapists have laughed in the faces of their victims and have held that they did them a favor. A person's acts do not exist in the abstract, in some strange realm, while he continues as an innocent man whom God supposedly requires us to love. The "love the sinner, hate the sin" idea goes back to Hellenic paganism and its virtual divorce of the body from the mind.

Modern man's love affair with the homosexual is really a hatred of God and a love affair with himself. He will answer, when challenged about his "concern" for homosexuals, that he has no use for them; he is concerned about their civil liberties; he wants a "free and open" society, and so on and so on. Of course, there is commonly an insistence that the Biblical texts about homosexuality refer to male prostitutes. Implicit in their reasoning is the premise, "If God tolerates them, He must certainly tolerate me!" One man said that he would like to be on our side, and would be if our affirmation of God and moral law were a more general one! Men and women have often insisted that they love their spouse, and their adulteries must be understood in context!

The total context of our lives is the triune God, His law-word, His atoning work in Christ, and more. If we do not take His law in all its facets seriously, we cannot appreciate His atoning work.

Chapter Twenty-Eight
The Golden Rule

17. Thou shalt not hate thy brother in thine heart: thou shalt in any wise rebuke thy neighbour, and not suffer sin upon him.
18. Thou shalt not avenge, nor bear any grudge against the children of thy people, but thou shalt love thy neighbour as thyself: I am the LORD. (Leviticus 19:17-18)

In the New Testament, we see the Golden Rule cited in Matthew 7:12; 22:35-40, and Luke 6:31. Our Lord tells us in Matthew 7:12, "this is the law and the prophets" (cf. Matt. 22:40). In other words, the essence of the law is the love of God and the love of our neighbor, so that *every* law given by God has this as its goal.

The love of our neighbor cannot be reduced to an emotion or a feeling. To love God means to obey His law. As our Lord tells us, "If ye love me, keep my commandments" (John 14:15). If we keep God's commandments, we thereby manifest our love towards Him. If we keep God's law with regard to our neighbor, we do not kill: we respect his life as God-given, not under our jurisdiction except in a God-given ordained court of law. We do not commit adultery to destroy his marriage: we respect its sanctity. We do not steal because we respect his property, nor do we bear false witness against him, thereby protecting his good name and God's law. Neither do we covet anything that is his, so that in word, thought, and deed, we manifest love towards him, for love is the fulfilling, or putting into force of the law (Rom. 13:8-9; Ex. 20:13-17). Our love of our neighbor means keeping God's law in relationship to him, and this is a powerful social force whereas our claim to an emotional love is usually a shallow deception, or at best a small thing compared to God's law.

To love our neighbor *as ourselves* means that we give him the same protection of God's law that we ourselves want. The peace and security of life and property which we want we give to others by placing God's law first. We are not the premise of social order, nor is our neighbor, but God is. We therefore can best express a love for our neighbor through our obedience to God's law.

No human penalty is attached to this law. Social disorder and anarchy are the God ordained penalties. But God both blesses and punishes more thoroughly than man can.

Before World War II, much use was made of the Golden Rule in public discourse. This has since ended, so that many are ignorant of what it was, and, in practice, there is too often a hostility to other people.

Chapter Twenty-Nine
A Holy Nation

The covenant people must establish a holy, covenant nation: Exodus 19:6; 22:31; 23:24f.; Leviticus 19:2; Deuteronomy 7:6; 14:2, 21; 26:18-19. In all their ways, God's people must manifest their holiness. Their every activity, to the very food they eat, must show that they have an unrestricted dedication and devotion to God and His law-word.

Here as elsewhere God gives no punitive power to man. Just as violation of the dietary laws brings its own penalties upon us, and just as a disregard for God's law limiting the extent of debt brings judgment upon us, so too a people's refusal to be a holy nation is its own punishment.

To be a holy nation means that God's purposes prevail over personal and national wishes. In Exodus 19:6, this means being "a kingdom of priests." A priest dedicates himself and all that he has to God's service. A nation must likewise be a holy nation.

Our holiness is apparent in the details of life. Thus, our diet must not include an animal, even if a clean one, that is torn by wild animals. Such meat must be given to the dogs (Ex. 22:31).

This also means no participation in pagan worship. Paganism cannot be allowed at any public function. Obedience here will bring health and prosperity, and the implication is that disobedience will bring the reverse (Ex. 23:24f.).

Because God is holy, we must be holy (Lev. 19:2). Holiness will bring the blessing of God (Deut. 7:6-11). God has *chosen* us by His grace and mercy; our actions must manifest our gratitude (Deut. 14:2-3, 21). We gain greatly by our covenant obedience (Deut. 26:18f.).

The emphasis in the idea of *a holy nation* is on God's grace, and then on our gratitude. Disobedience begins with the illusion that God's covenant law is a restraint upon a people's freedom rather than the ground of it. To see God's law as a limitation on us rather than our empowerment is the beginning of apostasy.

More than once in history, Christian nations have seen themselves as a new Israel of God. There is nothing wrong with this, and Paul in Galatians 6:16 sees the Christian community as "the Israel of God." That this concept has been abused does not diminish the fact that the churches and the nations are called to be God's chosen peoples and instruments.

Apart from this calling to be a holy nation, the various states pursue a course of self-aggrandizement, humanistic messiahship, and pragmatism. To be a holy nation means to see the priority of God and His law in all things, and to make true justice the goal of society.

Chapter Thirty
The Dietary Laws

1. The laws of unclean foods are given in Leviticus 11 and Deuteronomy 14.

2. The laws against eating blood are in Leviticus 19:26; Deuteronomy 12:23; 15:23; Leviticus 17:10-14.

3. Sacrificial meat permitted to the worshipper can only be eaten on the first two days after being offered and sacrificed: Leviticus 19:5-8; 7:15-19.

4. Neither fat nor blood can be eaten: Leviticus 3:17; 7:23-27.

5. No clean animal killed or torn by wild animals is to be eaten: it is to be given to the dogs: Exodus 22:31; Leviticus 7:24; 17:15; 22:8; Deuteronomy 14:21.

Over the years, I have seen considerable evidence of the rage of unbelievers against God's laws governing sexuality. Sex, for the humanists, is the area of freedom. Even men who are personally revolted at homosexuality will defend it as a major human right. For them, man, not God, must determine the use of one's sexuality.

For churchmen, a key area of resentment is the restriction on diet. The dietary laws are for them what God calls the forbidden foods, an abomination.

Although *obedience* to the dietary laws during the course of church history has been more extensive that realized, opposition to them has been intense. St. Gregory of Nyssa (c. 335 - c. 395 A. D.) turned all the laws of God into allegories, as he did also Biblical history.[1] His *status* as a saint is good evidence of the church's fallibility. Gregory held it to be unworthy of God to be concerned about foods, or law and history, for that matter. According to Gregory, "The Law does not instruct us how to eat. Nature which implants a desire for food in us is a sufficient lawgiver with regard to these things."[2]

The church is still full of men like Gregory, profoundly convinced of their saintliness as they rise above any need to heed God's laws concerning diet. Some have said that the concerns over such laws on my part are evidences of my lack of scholarly abilities. Well, faithfulness to God is for me the prized "ability."

These laws are the laws of *life*. We are summoned to choose life or death.

Of course, we do have the super-pious who are troubled over the necessity to eat and drink, urinate and defecate. One "holy" woman once remarked, or so it was reported to me, that she could not understand why God inflicted us with these bodily functions. He did so because He made us to be *creatures*, not co-gods!

---

[1] See Abraham J. Malherbe and Everett Ferguson, editors and translators, *Gregory of Nyssa: The Life of Moses* (New York, N.Y.: Paulist Press, 1978).
[2] *ibid.*, p. 78.

The dietary laws are reminders that we are creatures, if we need reminding. They tell us that the totality of our lives are to be governed by God and His word. It is the tempter who tells man, "Ye shall be as God" (Gen. 3:5), and it is the essence of sin to revolt against creatureliness. Those whose spirituality lifts them above the dietary laws are too spiritual for the God of the Bible.

God gives us guidelines to make life simpler and better for us, but we like to complicate everything and then whine about it. If you don't like the dietary laws, perhaps you don't like the God who gave them.

Chapter Thirty-One
Gossip and Speech

Gossip and false report are classified as false witness, or being "an unrighteous witness": Exodus 23:1-2; Leviticus 19:16; Deuteronomy 22:13-21. The references to Exodus 23:1-2, and Deuteronomy 22:13-21, have in mind a legal proceeding, although the case in Deuteronomy 22:13-21 begins as slander and becomes then legal action. Leviticus 19:16 refers to gossip. It is equated with taking a stand against a neighbor's life and is a very serous matter.

If one man assaults another, usually the bruises heal in a short time, but if he slanders his neighbor, the stain and hurt linger on. Hence it is that God so strongly stresses care in speech. In the Ten Commandments, the statement reads, "Neither shalt thou bear false witness against thy neighbour" (Deut. 5:20). The primary reference is to a court of law, but this does not exclude the court of life, where we continually bear witness before the Lord.

In the Sermon on the Mount, our Lord tells us, "But let your word Yes be Yes, and your No, No. Anything beyond this is from the evil one" (Matt. 5:37, Berkeley Version). He plainly connects gossip and trivializing speech as Satanic in inspiration, a very serious classification.

The Scriptures have much to say on speech. Paul in Colossians 4:6 declares, "Let your speech be alway with grace, seasoned with salt, that ye may know how ye ought to answer every man." Paul here speaks of the fact that a Christian may be attacked because of his faith. To answer all critics, one's speech should be "seasoned with salt," then an idiom for being intelligent and governed by wit rather than anger. Above all, one should always be governed by grace in speaking.

James 3:1-18 is a strong statement about the menace of an unruly tongue governed by malice and sin.

In brief, speech is a serious matter.

Chapter Thirty-Two
The Covenant Law

T. R. Hobbs has said, of law in the Bible, "All law presupposes the existence and identity of Israel's God, Yahweh, as the deliverer from Egypt."[1] The New Testament stresses the continuity with this in Matthew 5:17-20. Salvation is now more explicit: it is atonement, but the law as the way of life for the redeemed remains. Law-breaking is "a refusal to live within the relationship established by the covenant."[2] In other words, to reject the law of God is to reject the covenant and the covenant God in favor of an idol, a god created by man's imagination. Man's relationship to God is covenantal, and to attempt a direct relationship is to supplant Jesus Christ as mediator. Antinomians are implicitly replacing Christ with themselves.

Antinomians replace Jesus Christ with themselves. The word "covenant" is not in their vocabulary, although one at times can hear some speak of a very personal covenant with God, as though none other could exist.

A covenant between God and man is between a greater and a lesser party. In any such covenant, for the greater to enter into a covenant with a lesser party is *an act of grace*, so that a covenant by God with man is an act of sovereign and uncaused grace. But a covenant is a *treaty of law*, given by the greater, here by God, to the lesser, man, as the *way of life*. God gives His law to man as an act of grace so that man may have life rather than death.

A covenant is thus both grace and law when between God and man, as we see it in the Bible. It is a thoroughly relevant fact, given to determine what man's way of life should be under God. God's covenant is life, and the alternative is death.

But there is more. Man's life is on God's earth, and God's covenant is a *covenant of grant*, and as such it involves two things: a gift of land, and a status as the Great King's, or God's, man. (This kind of lord and client status existed in the medieval era.) God requires obedience, honor, and exclusive worship.[3]

Worship can be defined as obedience, faithfulness, service, fear, love, and full commitment to the covenant Lord.[4] In Deuteronomy 5:6-10, this requirement is clearly set forth:

> 6. I am the LORD thy God, which brought thee out of the land of Egypt, from the house of bondage.
> 7. Thou shalt have none other gods before me.
> 8. Thou shalt not make thee any graven image, or any likeness of any thing that is in heaven above, or that is in the earth beneath, or that is in the waters beneath the earth:

[1.] T. R. Hobbs: *Word Biblical Themes, 1, 2 Kings* (Dallas, Texas: Word Publishing, 1989), p. 32.
[2.] *ibid.*, p. 74.
[3.] *ibid.*, p. 48f.
[4.] *ibid.*, p. 50f.

9. Thou shalt not bow down thyself unto them, nor serve them: for I the LORD thy God am a jealous God, visiting the iniquity of the fathers upon the children unto the third and fourth generation of them that hate me,
10. And shewing mercy unto thousands of them that love me and keep my commandments.

First of all, God *requires* obedience to His law because, apart from the fact that He is our Creator, He is also our Redeemer. We owe Him obedience, now and forever. *Second*, this means, "Thou shalt have none other gods before me"; nothing else can have priority in our life: God alone is God, and God alone can be our God. *Third*, no graven image, whether the work of our hands *or of our minds*, can command our loyalty and worship. Today, many of our graven images are intellectual or institutional. As Alan Stang wrote, "Thou shalt have none other gods before me, including the state." *Fourth*, God is a jealous God: He requires exclusive worship. To give priority to anything else in our lives other than God is to deny Him. *Fifth*, God is a merciful God whose mercy extends down the generations to those who love Him. *Sixth*, God keeps His word. This is a great and encouraging fact, but also a terrifying one. God is not careless about records as we are, nor heedless or forgetful of what He has promised.

Law-keeping, life within the covenant, is living within the framework of God's covenant law. It means recognizing that we do not determine what our goodness consists of but that God and His law determine. He is the Lord, and all judgment rightfully belongs to Him.

It is always necessary to remember that the law is God's covenant law, given to us as an act of grace. Our response to grace, or the law given by grace, is not one of merit but of gratitude. For this reason, the Psalms strongly stress praise, thanksgiving, and gratitude as basic to our worship of God.

Chapter Thirty-Three
Law as Warfare

In Genesis 3:5 we encounter the Tempter's plan for mankind, every man as his own god, "knowing" or determining for himself what is good and evil, law and morality. This temptation is called *original sin* because, *first*, at the heart of all sin is the creature's will to be his own god and therefore determining for himself what constitutes good and evil. *Second*, it is called original sin because it is the first and key sin, the root of man's revolt against God. The fall of man is into this insistence on making all sin simply a relative matter, a question of personal choice, not of ultimate good and evil. This view has been made a matter of education's priority in our time. Most notably in the 1980s and 1990s, state schools, which barring Biblical teaching, have insisted in values-clarification teaching that "morality" does not deal with absolute good and evil but with purely personal and relative choices. Thus, it is held, homosexuality may be a "good" choice for one person but not another. Judgmentalism must be avoided, it is held, because "morality" is a matter of a personal life-style. Such a perspective is simply a present-day statement of Genesis 3:5, and it is basic to modern education.

It is an ancient heresy. Marcion's "good god" was superior because he was not judgmental, and he was against law, in particular the Law of the Bible and the Bible's God.[1] A long-standing vein of gnosticism within the church has held to this antinomianism. It has replaced the antithesis between good and evil with the neo-Manichean antithesis between spirit and matter. It has therefore affirmed antinomianism and transformed Christianity into another religion.

But the holy warfare of Scripture is not between spirit and matter. After all, Satan and his fallen angels are purely spiritual beings and yet totally evil. The holy warfare is a moral war, and the premise of the legions of God is the law of God. God's law tells us that good and evil are not relativistic terms but basic ones that describe and set forth a fundamental and unchanging difference. *The good* expresses God's holiness, righteousness or justice, knowledge, and dominion. These are communicable attributes of God which man must emulate, and this is done by obeying the law of God. The law of God tells us of His nature, so that we know God truly, though not exhaustively, in His law and His works.

In a college textbook on *Sexual Choices*, it is held that "self-respect and wholeness" should guide our "moral" decisions. Our choices should be "personal" not "social," and these imperatives should guide our personal

---

[1.] Joan P. Conliano, *The Tree of Gnosis* (San Francisco, California: Harper San Francisco, 1990), p. 153.

choices: equality, responsibility, and honesty. This means that objective and absolute standards are denied in favor of personal ones.[2]

Of course, this "free" and "liberated" sexuality is not free from the basic premise it wars against, Biblical morality. It regards God's moral law as the implicit or explicit enemy, and it has its own version of "the holy war"! Man to be free must wage war against God and His "repressive" laws.

All law is a form of warfare, including humanistic laws. Speed limits war against all who drive too fast or too recklessly. Failure to pay taxes is seen as an attack on the state's life and is severely punished. The state must have laws or go out of existence, and the life of the state depends on the people's obedience to the state and its laws.

God's law defends God's order. God's law sets forth God's justice, and obedience to it is necessary to the love and service of God. God's law tells us that there is a good and evil, and the Ten Commandments give us a summary of the law. The Sermon on the Mount defines the holy war more closely, and it requires our full obedience in word, thought, and deed. The difference between good and evil is not determined by man, nor by how certain acts affect us, but by the absolute and perfect Being of God. The premise for our obedience is given in Deuteronomy 6:4: "Hear, O Israel: The LORD our God is one LORD." There is a fundamental and total unity of being in the Godhead, no division, no disunity, and no conflict. When He speaks in and through His law, He gives us an undivided word and an unchanging requirement. God declares, "I am the LORD, I change not" (Mal. 3:6), which means that, because He is unchanging, so too is His law. Change and decay mark men and their ideas and works, but never God.

Life is a constant warfare. Men are at war with their past and present, and with one another. The world is not perfect, and they seek to change it to match their ideas of perfection. From the Christian perspective, the world is sinful and fallen and needs redemption and change, redemption by Christ's atonement, and then changed to conform to His law or justice.

The new creation does not abolish God's law any more than it sets aside the atonement. In the new creation the atoned live in the perfect justice or righteousness of God.

The antinomians who insist that they are not bound by God's law do not say the same about the state's law. They obey it, and, in so doing, they unite with the chief priests who said about Jesus, "We have no king but Caesar" (John 19:15). Which of these antinomians would welcome it if their children insisted that they were not bound by their parents' word? Or, insisted it was enough to "love" their parents, and that an insistence on obedience is legalism?

[2.] Gilbert D. Nass, Roger W. Libby, Mary Pat Fisher, *Sexual Choices, An Introduction to Human Sexuality* (Monterey, California: Wadsworth Health Sciences Division, (1981) 1984), p. 7.

Too much thinking in the church today is childish; it is resentful of any insistence on Biblical standards, and it is eclectic, picking and choosing from the Bible as though from a buffet table. But such a perspective is an insistence on man's autonomy from God. If we practice the Tempter's premise of Genesis 3:5 and insist on being our own god, it will not commend us to God if we at times use His word to buttress our word and our independence.

As Cornelius Van Til stated it, the choice is between autonomy (self-law) and theonomy (God's law).

Chapter Thirty-Four

Sin

Ernest F. Kevan pointed out some years ago that God's law defines sin. It follows, therefore, "If there is sin there also must be Law, for sin is transgression of law (1 John iii.4)."[1] God's law is much more than a legal code: it is covenantal law. It establishes a personal relationship between God and man. For this reason, disobedience to God's law is regarded by the prophets as adultery, as a betrayal of a close union. It is thus much more than breaking a law or violating a statute. It is the most fundamental kind of disloyalty one can commit. It is a personal affront to God the Lord, a betrayal precisely where the most intense loyalty should exist.

The Biblical (Hebrew) word *hesed* means loyal kindness, loving-kindness, and even love. *Hesed* presupposes the covenant, a relationship where man should manifest the most intense kind of loyalty. The word occurs 128 times in the Psalms.

> *Hesed* is eternal (Ps. 105; 106; 117; 135); characterized by fidelity (Ps. 84:11; 88; 137:8); immensity (Ps. 32; 35:6; 56:11; 102:11; 107:5); fullness (Ps. 35:6-11); and reveals God's beneficent saving spirit (Ps. 6:5; 30:17; 50:3). Ps. 97:2-3 which "hails the saving quality of Hesed" is "the Liturgy's Christmas song to celebrate the birth of Jesus, which means Savior." In addition the divine *hesed* is marked by humility of love "which stoops to equality with its beloved and even to the lower self-abasement of the 'form of a slave' (Phil. 2:7)." Consequently God showers his *hesed* upon the poor and humble (Ps. 67, 71). The omnipotent power and justice that mark God's *hesed* (Ps. 61:12f.) make it possible for God to give victory to the weak and poor and to laugh at the futility of creature self-exaltation (Ps. 2; 36:13; etc.). Simultaneously God is quick to pardon (Ps. 29:6). [2]

Hesed on the part of man means faithfulness of men one to another, and towards God. It means the knowledge of God and the fear of God; it means "religiosity, piety, kindness, and love of mankind." It means mercy and compassion and more because it expressed a loyalty to the covenant, and it is an expression of covenant life.[3] On God's part, *hesed* expresses His covenantal fellowship; it expresses His covenant grace in helping us.[4]

In Micah 6:8 God's primary requirement of man, in Moffatt's rendering, is "to be just and kind, and live in quiet fellowship with your God." This is "God's first inescapable requirement...that the Israelites do 'justice,' Hebrew *mishpat*, a common term for the legal norms demanded by the covenant.[5] The second requirement of Micah 6:8 is to love mercy, or to be kind, i.e., *hesed*.

[1.] Ernest F. Kevan: *The Moral Law* (Jekintown, Pennsylvania: Sovereign Grace Publishers, 1963), p. 88.
[2.] *Hesed in the Bible* (Cincinnati, Ohio: The Hebrew Union College Press, 1967), p. 18f.
[3.] *ibid.,* p. 69.
[4.] *ibid.,* p. 102.

The curses pronounced in the Bible are for contempt for and disregard of God's law. One does not escape the curses by denying the Law that proclaims them.

Pietism has tended to reduce God's relationship to mankind to a non-covenantal and purely personal one. Abraham knew better. In Genesis 18:17ff., God tells Abraham of the impending judgment on Sodom and Gomorrah for their wickedness. This Abraham does not deny; his concern is with the innocent. Will they also be judged? God answers Abraham saying that He will spare Sodom if ten righteous men can be found. Judgment must come, but a righteous element, upholding justice, can avert it. Responsibility is not purely personal: we have a responsibility to the country and the place of our residence. The law speaks to our total life. Thus, in Deuteronomy 21:1-9, we have a law regarding a murdered man found in a field. The city closest to the dead man must assume responsibility for his death. If the murderer cannot be found, then a heifer must be sacrificed to make atonement for the unsolved murder. In other words, every wrong must be righted; if not on earth, then God in His judgments in history and at the Last Judgment will complete the righting of all wrongs.

What this tells us about sin is that it is a very personal affront to the triune God. An impersonal statist law is constantly broken, often with impunity, and the many violations are in time forgotten because perfect enforcement is not even dreamed. God's law presupposes full and perfect enforcement. What God does not complete in time and history is enforced in hell. The necessary requirement of justice is restitution, recompense, repayment. Disbelief in hell means in time a disbelief in justice, and a pessimism with regard to history.

God's covenant with man is not only a gift of law but a gift of *land*. Tenure on the land is *normally* in return for covenantal obedience. Thus to despise and disobey God's law is an invitation to displacement and captivity. Associated with this is God's curse upon covenant-breakers by means of bad weather and natural disasters (drought, flood, earthquake, etc.), and by means of an inflicted judicial blindness. Blindness to God's law is a blindness to reality.

[5.] Delbert R. Hillers, *Covenant: The History of a Biblical Idea* (Baltimore, Maryland: The Johns Hopkins Press, 1969), p. 130.

Chapter Thirty-Five
"The Salt of the Earth"

Early in 1996, an incident occurred which opened my eyes to a sad fact. About six or eight of our Chalcedon fellowship were eating together at a restaurant. We began with prayer as usual. (If the place is too noisy, we have silent prayer.) When we finished praying, a man at another table came over to thank us for praying! I suddenly realized that I could not recall when I last saw other people praying at a restaurant, and it distressed me.

Our Lord, in Matthew 5:13-14, requires us to be the salt of the earth and the light of the world. The use of salt over the centuries has been primarily as a preservative, to keep food usable prior to refrigeration's invention. In my lifetime, as a boy, our cellar had crocks which kept fish and cheese in a brine. Later, on the Indian Reservation, I preserved trout and beef in the same way. We are required by Our Lord to keep the world from radical corruption by being salt, while we strive to bring men and nations to Christ by being light to the world.

The early church recognized this duty and created the diaconate to care for widows, orphans, the needy, and more; Christian schooling; courts of arbitration and settlement (1 Cor. 6:1ff.); and much, much more. In 1592, a letter from the early church was published; the author was unknown, and Diognetus, to whom the letter was addressed, was also unknown. The writer referred to himself as "a disciple of the apostles," and he speaks of Christianity as being a *new* thing in the world. In Chap. V of the letter, the writer describes the Christians as the abused but preserving power among the peoples. In Chap. VI, we are told that Christians are the soul of the world, i.e., "what the soul is in the body, that are Christians in the world," its life-giving power.

> The soul is imprisoned in the body, yet preserves that very body; and Christians are confined in the world as a prison, and yet they are the preservers of the world.[1]

This, then, is the designated purpose of the Christian in the world according to Christ the Redeemer-King. If the Christian fails in this task, corruption will take over the world and make of it another Sodom and Gomorrah.

In 1996, the United States has millions of evangelical Christians. Those over 18 in age who said that they were born again and believe the Bible from cover to cover had grown to c. 91 million persons, very much more than the numbers of 1968. In the years since 1968, abortion and homosexuality have been legalized, and euthanasia virtually so. The impotence of these church peoples is startling. If they do not have "courage" to pray in public, how can they be the

---

[1.] "The Epistle to Diognetus," in Roberts, Donaldson, and F. Crombie, translators, *The Writing of the Apostolic Fathers* (Edinburgh, Scotland: T. & T. Clark, 1867).

salt of the earth, or any light to it? If they neither practice nor affirm God's law, of what good are they but to be cast out and trodden under foot of man? (Matt. 5:13)

The world has always had its share of sin, but now crimes are like a tidal wave. A few articles from one newspaper will illustrate this. The chairwoman of a county housing authority was being forced out of office because of a "decade-old conviction for embezzlement of federal housing money."[2] On the night of July 21, 1995, seven teenagers roamed the streets of Stockton, it was alleged, looking for a prostitute to gang-rape and kill, torturing her in the process.[3] A high school social studies teacher in Sacramento, age 38, is alleged to have murdered his wife and left her body with the two terrified children for weeks while he fled.[4]

More such accounts can be cited. True, vicious crimes have always occurred, but earlier in this century, such crimes were not commonplace, and now they are. Christians have ceased to be salt and light in too many cases. It has been said that, after World War II, homosexuals came out of the closet, and Christians retreated into it.

Christians are called to dominion (Gen. 1:26-28). The creation or dominion mandate has not become obsolete but more relevant than ever. But the church has been turned into a convent into which tender souls flee from the world, to await either the rapture or the sad end of the world, depending on what they believe. Will the Lord want such cowardly souls who dare not even pray in public?

The law is God's plan for victory and dominion. The law is the expression of God's nature and being: it sets forth His righteousness or justice. To reject God's law is to reject God and to worship an idol made out of our own imagination. We may use Biblical materials to create our idol, ("God is love"), but it is still an idol. The living God is all that He declares Himself to be in His word, no less and no more than He is.

[2.] Ann Schnyder, "Old conviction prompts insurers to drop S.J. commission chief," in *The Record,* (Stockton, California), Wednesday, October 16, 1996, p. 1.

[3.] Cindy Sui, "'Lost Little Boys' and a Brutal Slaying," *The Record,* (Stockton, California), Sunday, August 4, 1996, p. 1.

[4.] "Kids live weeks with mom's body," *The Record,* (Stockton, California), Tuesday, October 15, 1996, p. A1, A8.

Chapter Thirty-Six
No Grace, No Law

As we have seen, there is no freedom without law, God's in particular. Antinomianism denies the validity of moral absolutes. At best, it reduces good and evil to relative rather than moral concerns. Because antinomianism removes the restraints on man and on all human agencies, it empowers them to play God (Gen. 3:5) and to seek to establish the determinative power in themselves. Antinomianism says in effect that all actions and thoughts are permissible and acceptable, and it reduces morality to a personal "life style."

Not only is there no freedom without law, there is also no law of God without grace. It is God's grace that gives to us a covenant status, and a covenant from God is a gift of law. God's law reveals to us the way of life, and God's redemptive grace in and through Jesus Christ enables us to obey God's law, not perfectly but essentially. In Christ, we become the people of God's law, which is now also written in the tables of our hearts (Jer. 31:31-34). God's people are marked by a covenantal faith: they believe and obey God's every word.

Men are too prone today to attempts to dissect God, to separate His love from law, and His grace from wrath, and to isolate heaven from hell, salvation from judgment, and so on and on. Whether such attempts are after the pattern of the Abbot Joachim of Flora or modern dispensationalism, they are dangerously in error. In every age, God the Lord is the same: "For I am the LORD, I change not" (Mal. 3:6). To deny any aspect of God's being is to deny all of it; it means denying God. As a man, a redeemed sinner, I have diverse and sometimes conflicting aspects in my being, but not so God. God has no need, as do you and I, to outgrow certain character traits. There are not conflicting aspects to God's being, and to assume that there are becomes anthropomorphic thinking.

Instead of seeking to isolate and separate the various attributes of God into conflicting forces, we need to see the simplicity and unity of God's being. Then we can say, with Derek Carlsen, "Love means to obey."

> The greatest commandment is to love God with all our heart, soul, mind and strength (Matt. 22:36-40), and real love is shown by obeying everything that God says (John 14:15; 1 John 5:3; Luke 6:46; Matt. 7:22-23). Would Adam and Eve love God by living in obedience to His Word? Would they find their joy, peace and happiness in obeying and loving their Creator? Would they find fulfillment in who they were under God or would they look for this somewhere else? Would they be content with the fact that they were made by God and therefore, could never be equal with God? Would they be prepared to get all of their knowledge and understanding of everything from God? Would they interpret everything in the light of what God said about it, or would they seek to be the final authority and interpret everything independently from God? Would they willingly and lovingly

submit to their Creator? The simple test that God had set before them would give answers to all of these questions.[1]

Men seek fulfillment, either under God, or apart from God. It is a course of impotence to use God's name while seeking independence from Him, and this too many churchmen have done and do. A basic premise of such compromised thinking is self-justification. We expect this from the enemies of Christ. From His ostensible people, this is blasphemy. To define God apart from his law-word is to create a god in our own image.

We can add further that there is no grace without law. Grace manifests God's mercy to us; by grace we are included within God's Kingdom, made members of His new creation. Grace therefore gives us God's law. As one man said, after his conversion, suddenly the woman he was passionately attached to adulterously became alien and repulsive to him. Without having yet heard of theonomy, he knew he was now under God's law by God's grace.

God's saving grace makes us a new creation in Christ (2 Cor. 5:17). Grace *commands* us. Paul in 2 Corinthians 10:15f. tells the Corinthians that, as their faith grows, it will provide more abundantly for his support and to enable him to preach the Gospel in lands that lie beyond them. Grace commands; it leads to growth in obedience and faithfulness. A lawless grace is no grace at all.

N. H. Smith has written of *grace*, "The main and characteristic N.T. use of the word grace (Gr. *charis*) is of God's redemptive love which is always active to save sinners and maintain them in proper relationship with him."[2] The "proper relationship" with God is faithfulness to the covenant law. Grace is the free gift of God, and obedience to God's covenant law is the necessary response of the faithful.

Because the law is given as an act of grace by God's covenant favor, it is essentially a part of the Gospel. It is good news because it tells us what life in our Lord means. It is good news because it is our way of life in our redeeming Lord.

The antinomians have so abused God's law that some have actually taught that it was somehow given by the devil, which means an implicit or explicit rejection of the Old Testament and an affirmation of Marcionism.

Is it any wonder that the churches are largely impotent? The word of God is one word. To subtract from that unified one word is to alter, subvert, and to change that word into another. Such abuses of Scripture are commonplace. In the first half of the 19th century, an American circuit-rider, with a strong dislike for a female hairstyle that had coils of hair piled on top of a woman's head, preached a sermon against it. Supposedly, Jesus had railed against the same style, saying, "Topknot, come down!" His text was Matthew 24:17: "Let him which is

---

[1.] Derek Carlsen, *Faith and Reason, The First Steps to Christian Maturity* (Reason of Hope Ministries, P.O. Box 3348, Paulington, Mutare, Zimbabwe, 1996), p. 21.

[2.] N. H. Smith, "Grace," in Alan Richardson: *A Theological Word Book of the Bible,* (New York, N. Y.: The Macmillan Co., (1950) 1960), p. 101.

on the housetop not come down." Is this insane "interpretation" any worse than the many sermons on Matthew 5:17-20 which attempt to "prove" that our Lord set aside the Law in these words that stress its eternity? We may not like what God has to say, but this does not give us the right to falsify it. Which is worse, to *break* certain specific laws, or to *deny* the whole of the law?

Chapter Thirty-Seven
"Yea, Hath God Said?"

In January, 1974, Marshall Berman, a member of the political science department at City College, CUNY, wrote a perceptive essay on "Sympathy for the Devil: Faust, the '60s and the Tragedy of Development."[1] His very able analysis saw the motivation behind the 1960s student revolutionary movement, of which he was a part. In part, it had the spirit of the Doors, a singing group, whose song, "We want the world, and we want it — NOW!", was very much in tune with the times. Another aspect of many was the NAY-saying spirit. To oppose the powers that be was seen as equivalent to virtue.

In Genesis 3:1, the tempter raises the question to Eve, "Yea, hath God said?" Strength and virtue are equated by the tempter with NAY-saying, and the NAY is the essence of freedom.

Over the centuries, the NAY-sayers have been many, and they have accused the YEA-sayers of being mindless. However, as we read these NAY-sayers, such as Shelley, Byron, and Blake, we see an amazing mindlessness on their part. To say NAY to the wisdom of God is not an instant certificate of wisdom, nor does it reflect anything but an enthronement of sin as virtue.

The premise of such NAY-saying is that God cannot be right, and that rebellion, instead of being wrong, is freedom and deliverance from tyranny. For God to declare laws that man never gave his assent to is seen as an assault on man's dignity and freedom.

Now the premise of Scripture is that man was created in the image of God, in knowledge, holiness, righteousness (or justice) and dominion (Gen. 1:27f.; Col. 3:10; Eph. 4:24). Man is God's creation and creature, totally derivative and unoriginal. The only thing original about man is his sin, and even that is an aspect of God's eternal decree. But man seeks originality and freedom, and he believes this is attainable by rebellion against God. It means challenging God's law-word: "Yea, hath God said?"

Law expresses God's nature, eternal, unchanging and totally good, so that God's law is justice. Because God defines justice or righteousness, the rebel against God must deny God's definition. Man is of time, and laws must be also; they must be seen, fallen man holds, as expedient instruments for short-term goals. Man is to be free from law to realize his own being as unbound by anything external to himself. Existentialism is a modern philosophy which fully expresses this faith. The self-realization of man thus means his awareness of himself apart from God, as a separate and free being who defines himself. Since man's self-definition is in defiance of God, it is a non-definition because man

---

[1.] *American Review 19, The Magazine of New Writing,* January, 1974, pp. 23-75.

refuses to accept any *given* or *a priori* definition of himself. Man must make and define himself, but this self-definition must be in contempt of God.

Moses, confronted by God in the wilderness, is bewildered by what God is: where has God been since the days of the patriarchs? Who is God, and what is His *Name*, His definition? But God refuses to define Himself as other than "I AM THAT I AM," or I am He who Is, the eternally self-existent God (Ex. 3:13f.). Then, however, God declares that He is the God of Abraham, Isaac, and Jacob; He is known through His self-revelation (Gen. 3:15). He is known truly although not exhaustively in His self-revelation because there are no contradictions in His being.

But the essence of man's expression of himself is *contradiction*. He is made in the image of God, and every atom of his being reveals God, so that the things visible and invisible of God are all known to him (Rom. 1:19-21). Man is a walking revelation of God, but also a walking denial of Him because, as a sinner, he is totally given to the rejection of his Creator. God's law is therefore anathema to man because his self-definition requires the rejection of God's law and word. "Yea, hath God said?" is basic to man's fallen nature, and his premise is, "I will have none other God than myself." At times, men have formalized their rebellion into a ritual, declaring, "As my will is, so must it be." They often use religion and the church to express their secret hatred of God, and they see themselves as the wise ones of history.

But nothing has changed. God's law still prevails, and it judges men and nations.

Chapter Thirty-Eight
Law

The Hebrew word *torah*, and the Greek word *nomos*, had in origin somewhat different meanings, but, as the New Testament uses *nomos*, it clearly is not far from *torah*. The problem with *law* is not a discrepancy in meaning between Old and New Testaments but between the Bible and modern usage. Thus, one dictionary definition of law states that law is "a binding custom or practice of a community: a rule of conduct or action prescribed or normally recognized as binding or enforced by a controlling authority." This definition is sociological and political. Certainly there are folk customs and statist laws that fit this definition, but this is like defining a *man* as: an Englishman, American, or Italian; true enough but very limited, parochial, and misleading. Law is essentially religious; it sets forth what is basic to the nature of being because it comes from the being of God. There can be bad laws, laws made by men and civil governments, but the fact of bad laws does not nullify the validity nor meaning of law. There can be good and bad definitions of physical data, such as gravity, but false definitions do not eliminate the fact that something real is being described.

God's law is covenantal, so that it is both a gift of His grace and also law, a way of life given by God in His mercy. As W. A. Whitehouse wrote, "The Law was, in the first instance, an *offer* of life after a prescribed and blessed pattern. To men who cannot or will not accept what is offered in the word of God, it becomes a stern command."[1]

Law is always a *command* word, and, as Whitehouse has noted, "The complementary term for command is *promise*."[2] It is *promise* because the law is to the obedient a form of grace. Thus, as our Lord sums up the law, He tells us, in Mark 12:29-31:

> 29. ...The first of all the commandments is, Hear, O Israel; The LORD our God is one Lord:
> 30. And thou shalt love the Lord thy God with all thy heart, and with all thy soul, and with all thy mind, and with all thy strength: this is the first commandment.
> 31. And the second is like, namely this, Thou shalt love thy neighbour as thyself. There is none other commandment greater than these.

The purpose of the law is to teach us the love of God, and then the love of our neighbor. The whole of human society is thus bound together under God in the common service of God and in care one for another. All the specific regulations of the law serve these two purposes. If we take the specific laws in isolation from

---

[1] W. A. Whitehouse, "Law," in Alan Richardson, editor: *A Theological Word Book of the Bible* (New York, N.Y.: Macmillan, (1950) 1960), p. 124.
[2] W. A. Whitehouse, "Command," in *ibid.*, p. 50. Whitehouse's perspective differs from this writer's.

the covenant, and the two great functions of the law, we will see them as restraints upon us rather than as blessings.

How then can ostensible Christians see the law as alien to our faith when it is given by God as the means of blessing us? It is an ugly matter when the enemies of God curse Him and His law. Is it not much more offensive to Him when His supposed people do so? First Peter 4:17 tells us that "judgment must begin at the house of God," and this is certainly most true throughout the Old Testament and culminating with the fall of Jerusalem in the Jewish-Roman war of A. D. 66-70. Will not the judgment of the church be a fearful one if it continues to show contempt for God's law?

Citing Whitehouse once again, he called attention to "the N. T. use of *dogma*, a word properly translated as ordinance. It is used of imperial decrees, and of ordinances decreed by the Apostles and Elders in Jerusalem (Acts 17:7 and 16:4)."[3] (The Greek word from whence *dogma* had its origin has as its meaning *to think*. Dogma thus means the apprehension of the rationale and meaning of things.)

God's laws, commands, ordinances, or dogmas thus set forth the meaning and rationale of life in the Lord. Proverbs 16:25 tells us, "There is a way that seemeth right unto a man, but the ends thereof are the ways of death." *Way* is in the Hebrew *derek*, a road, a way of life or a course of action. This is what God's law is, but it is, unlike man's fallen way, the way of faithfulness and obedience, of justice or righteousness. The law is given as God's blessing, the established path for life. To denigrate law is to denigrate life itself. The two *ways* were strongly affirmed by the early church. In Psalm 1:6, we have the clear statement of the two ways, the way of the righteous, and the way of the ungodly. The godly find their delight "in the law of the LORD" (Ps. 1:2). So it should be now.

---

3. Whitehouse, "Statute, Ordinances," in *ibid.*, p. 247.

Chapter Thirty-Nine
Limited Atonement

The doctrine of limited atonement has an important relationship to God's law. According to this dogma, God's atonement through the atoning sacrifice of Jesus Christ was for His elect people. It was efficacious because those whom He died to save are indeed saved by God's sovereign grace.

The doctrine of unlimited atonement, common to Arminianism, holds that Christ's sacrifice made salvation available to all who choose to be saved and who accept Jesus Christ as their Lord and Savior. As one man who advocated unlimited atonement held, together with countless others, Christ's atoning blood is like money in the bank for the fallen race of men. Any and all who are ready to accept Jesus Christ as Lord and Savior can then immediately draw on their account in the bank and become redeemed.

This Arminian view places the initiative in salvation in man's hands. Man need only draw on his account and salvation is applied to him. In this perspective, sovereignty in salvation is transferred from God to man. Grace is not so much grace as an available asset. Instead of God's law as the way of sanctification, enthusiasm replaces it as the mark of faith. The law is attacked as legalism, and revivalism is used to recharge men with grace. One man who loved revival meetings said that he had been "saved" at least a dozen times from his backsliding, by which he meant that sanctification as well as salvation were essentially emotional affirmation and zeal.

The root of the problem goes back to the meaning of *forgiveness*. We *cannot* understand the Biblical meaning of the word unless we begin with the fact that in the Old Testament it is inseparable from the sacrificial system, and, in the New Testament, from Christ's atonement, in its essential meaning. In relationship to God, it requires sacrifice, i.e., the death penalty as restitution, with the animals sacrificed as types of God's Redeemer and His sacrifice. In relationship to God, "without shedding of blood is no remission" of sin (Heb. 9:22). The atonement by Jesus Christ was a *necessity* for the remission of our sins against God.

Exodus 22 gives us the requirement for the remission of sins against man, restitution, from twofold to fivefold. The penalty in some instances, as for murder, is death as our restitution.

By separating *forgiveness* from sacrifices of atonement and from restitution, we have reduced its meaning from a legal or juridical requirement to a matter of emotions. Few revolutions in history have been more deadly than the shift in theology from God's law to man's emotions. Forgiveness now means, "*I* forgive you," i.e., I am no longer angry with you. It has nothing to do with the offender's repentance and restitution and hence nothing to do with God's law.

The Biblical meaning of *forgiveness* is clearly seen in St. Paul, for whom it is inseparably linked with *justification. Feeling* has nothing to do with it, whereas God's law is inseparable from it. In Jesus Christ, man is a *pardoned* sinner (Rom. 8:1) and a new creature. The Greek word, *aphiemi*, remit, has at root a *legal* meaning: "to release from a legal bond (office, guilt, etc.) and also a woman from a marriage." Also, "Sometimes it stands for *kipper*, to cover, make atonement (Isa. 22:14)."[1]

Clearly, *forgiveness* in the Bible is not a blanket remission nor is it without cost *to the forgiven.* Arminian forgiveness leaves all the penalty on Jesus Christ, and a self-willed view of gaining remission with the sinner. It transfers priority and sovereignty from God to man. No judge sits on a bench merely to give to the guilty men before him whatever they want!

Limited atonement upholds the sovereignty of God and His law. It does not supplant God's law with man's emotional responses. We are told in John 10:11, 15 that Jesus Christ died for "his sheep"; in Acts 20:28, for "his church"; for the "elect" according to Romans 8:32-35; and for "his people" (Matt. 1:21). His atonement was for all races and classes of men, not all men without exception.

Unlimited atonement sets aside the meaning of forgiveness in its Biblical and juridical sense to give it a lawless meaning. Antinomianism and unlimited atonement go together. Because unlimited atonement has prevailed, we have seen a shift from theology to anthropology, from a God-centered to a man-centered stress in the churches. The result is scarcely Christianity. Not surprisingly, a prominent Arminian "theologian" of the 1930s held that the atonement was basically a mystery; he could not view it except in antinomian terms and hence it had lost its meaning for him.

Any weakening of God's law is also a weakening of the meaning of the atonement. We have seen a steady loss of meaning for the doctrine of the atonement as antinomianism has prevailed. But without the atonement there is no Christianity.

---

[1] H. Vorlander, "Forgiveness," in Colin Brown, general editor: *The New International Dictionary of New Testament Theology,* vol. I, (Grand Rapids, Michigan: Zondervan, 1975), p. 698. See also N. H. Smith, "Forgiveness," in Alan Richardson, editor: *A Theological Word Book of the Bible* (New York, N.Y.: Macmillan, (1950) 1960), p. 86.

Chapter Forty
The Family

Of the Ten Commandments, four are concerned with the protection of the family: 1) "Honor thy father and thy mother"; 2) "Thou shalt not commit adultery"; 3) "Thou shalt not steal"; 4) "Thou shalt not covet thy neighbour's house, thou shalt not covet thy neighbour's wife, nor his manservant, nor his maidservant, nor his ox, nor his ass, nor any thing that is thy neighbour's" (Ex. 20:12, 14, 15, 17). Clearly, the family is of central importance to God. While the Bible has many references to God which invoke other images and concepts, such as shepherd and king, the most important title comes from the family. God calls Himself "Our Father" (Matt. 6:9) to best explain His relationship to us. We are His children by the adoption of grace.

The family is the center of life, its nursery and sanctuary. The father has authority, and this authority is one that includes providing sustenance and protecting life. To call a man "father" means to submit to his authority. In 2 Kings 8:9, when Ben-hadad, king of Syria, was sick, he asked of the prophet Elisha whether or not he would recover. In so asking, Ben-hadad spoke of himself as "Thy son Ben-hadad of Syria." By this he indicated that he would submit to the authority of God and His prophet Elisha.

Our Lord emphasized the meaning of the law concerning the family and attacked the Pharisees for undermining the law with their interpretations:

> 9. And he said unto them, Full well ye reject the commandment of God, that ye may keep your own tradition.
> 10. For Moses said, Honour thy father and thy mother; and, Whoso curseth father or mother, let him die the death:
> 11. But ye say, If a man shall say to his father or mother, It is Corban, that is to say, a gift, by whatsoever thou mightest be profited by men: he shall be free.
> 12. And ye suffer him no more to do ought for his father or his mother;
> 13. Making the word of God of none effect through your tradition, which ye have delivered: and many such like things do ye.
> (Mk. 7:9-13)

Supposedly, a gift to God negated the need to support one's parents. Our Lord does not allow this Pharisaic evasion of family responsibility to stand. He equates it with cursing one's parents, the penalty for which is death in Exodus 21:17. There is thus a strong emphasis in the New Testament on the family and its authority (Eph. 6:1-4).

At the same time, it is clear that the earthly family cannot supplant the heavenly. Our Lord declares, "And call no man your father upon the earth; for one is your Father, which is in heaven" (Matt. 23:9). This sentence follows Matthew 23:1-8, an attack on the false pretension to authority on the part of the Pharisees. It tells us that the fatherly authority is primarily and essentially from

God, not from men who claim to speak for God. It is not a prohibition of the use of the word "father" but of religious attempts to arrogate human and divine authority to men.

Jesus Christ is the truly obedient son (Hosea 11:1; Matt. 2:15). The Father gives full authority to the Son (John 3:35; 5:22-23; 16:15), but no church nor man can claim such an authority.

Out of this Biblical usage has come the custom, still common to some churches, of addressing fellow Christians as "brother" and "sister."

The law of God was given to the covenant people, not as a mass of persons, but as families with an established pattern of authority and government. The *father* had a duty to teach his family the full meaning of God's law (Deut. 6:2), because the law is a catechism of life.

It is customary on the part of modern writers to depict the family as a narrow, ingrown entity. This is emphatically not Biblical. However close the family ties, the laws against consanguinity ensured the Biblical family from such fate. With each marriage, the relationships were extended outward.

This fact is very important. The family is God's basic governmental institution. The family, with each generation, moves outward by marriage, and the interlocking network of law units is thereby spread further. The family governs itself, and, in so doing, its government covers many spheres of life and its future orientation means that its functions are not present-bound. Over the centuries, families have most tenaciously preserved past and present while working to govern the future.

Because the family is the womb of life, it is also the locale of basic government. It is man's first church and state, his first school and vocation, the first economic realm, and more. The further away from the family that man's basic government is placed, the more dangerous it becomes. Sometimes the church, and certainly the modern state, seeks to arrogate to itself powers which properly belong to the family. The result is the impoverishment of society.

Chapter Forty-One
Elders and Government

The term *elders* tells us at once that government in God's law is, *first*, family oriented. The term refers to a man of advanced age who is the head of a household and has proven his ability to rule well by his government therein. He must be able to rule his own house before being entrusted with authority elsewhere (1 Tim. 3:5). The Bible is inescapably patriarchal. The qualifications of an elder in the New Testament simply restate Old Testament law and practice (1 Tim. 3:1-13; 5:1, etc.).

Second, elders of various varieties existed, governing specific areas of life. There are the elders of a people, as of Israel, Judah, Moab, and Midian (Num. 22:4, 7), and of Egypt (Gen. 50:7). There are elders of an area, as of Gilead (Judges 11:5-11), and the elders of a tribe (Deut. 31:28). In Jeremiah 29:1, Jeremiah writes to the elders who are in captivity as still leaders of the people, together with priests and prophets. There were also elders for specific groups, such as priests (2 Kings 19:2; Jer. 19:1). There were elders for the city, elders for the "house" (i.e., palace), as in Genesis 50:7 and 2 Samuel 12:17.

There were *elders of the city*, whose work included the protection of the family. Five laws refer to them specifically for decision: 1) blood redemption (Deut. 19:12); 2) the expiation of an unsolved murder (Deut. 21: 3, 6); 3) the case of the incorrigible son (Deut. 21:19); 4) the defamation of a virgin (Deut. 22:15); and 5) the law of the levirate (Deut. 25:9).

There were also *the elders of the people or country*, i.e., of the state. In 1 Kings 20:7, even so powerful a king as Ahab consulted these leaders before proclaiming war. The elders later on worked with Elisha against the king (2 Kings 6:32).

According to Louis Isaac Rabinowitz, the function of the elders of the people were, *first*, to represent the people in the covenant with God, and in the proclamation of the law (Ex. 19:7; 24:9; Deut. 27:1; 29:10; 31:9; Josh. 8:33; 24:1). *Second*, to appoint a leader, military or civil, to rule over the people (Judges 11:5-11; 1 Sam. 8:4). *Third*, the elders also formally declare war (Josh. 8:10; 2 Sam. 17:4-15). *Fourth*, political negotiations and treaties were their duty (Ex. 3:16, 18; 4:29; Num. 16:25; 2 Sam. 3:17; 5:3). *Fifth*, religious ceremonies were their duty (Ex. 12:21; 18:12; Lev. 9:1; 1 Sam. 4:3; 1 Kings 8:1, 3; 1 Chron. 15:25). *Sixth*, they acted in times of national crises (Ex. 17:5-6; Josh. 7:6; 1 Sam. 4:3; 1 Chron. 21:16).[1]

Although government by family elders was first suggested to Moses by his father-in-law, Jethro, it was adopted by Moses because God so ordered it. The families of Israel were divided into tens, fifties, hundreds, and thousands. Elders

---

[1] Louis Isaac Rabinowitz, "Elders," in *Encyclopaedia Judaica*, vol. 6 (Jerusalem, Israel: Kater Publishing House, 1971), pp. 578ff.

were chosen over each group from tens on up, and they were judges in all cases within their jurisdiction, or, on appeal, to their higher court. At the top were the seventy elders who worked under Moses.

This pattern was used in the church. The seventy cardinals of the Church of Rome, commonly laymen at the time, had ruling powers. The hundreds courts were once common to Christendom, and the American colonies had them also.

Thus, in church and state, rule by elders was once the practice. This meant that, instead of government from the top down, government from the family level was once the standard and sometimes the practice.

In the 20th century, the popular myth of democracy has convinced many that it is rule by the people when in practice the triumph of democracy has meant a radical concentration of power at the top in the name of the people. Democracy has also placed law-making in the hands of a ruling class at the top. As a result, we have seen a remarkable concentration of power in the name of the people.

Freedom is a myth, however, unless it begins with the self-government of the people as persons. What we have in its stead is license, the license to abort, practice euthanasia, commit sodomy, and more, manifestations not of freedom but of sin and slavery.

In 1973, an interesting essay was written by one who had been a student rebel of the 1960s. It was entitled "Sympathy for the Devil: Faust, the '60s and the Tragedy of Development." The devil is a destroyer, and he wills to destroy God's works of creation. The spirit of permissiveness which marked this movement from the 1960s on was a spirit of destruction, of negation to the creative and affirmation to the destructive. (In the early years of abortion, some women got pregnant in order to have an abortion and thereby join the ranks of the liberated.) This spirit meant rejecting the belief "that good can only follow from good, and evil only from evil," as naive and foolish.[2]

This perspective rejects causality. In its decline, Greece lost in its popular writings a sense of cause and effect, and this prepared the way for the Thirty Tyrants. So too now the sense of causality is gone, as popular literature so clearly gives us evidence of, and the ability to understand leaves the people. Men do in practice seem to believe that they can gather figs from thistles, as Edna St. Vincent Millay affirmed in defiance of Jesus (Matt. 7:16).

Where government is weak or absent on the personal level, it will soon turn into tyranny. Attempts at reform are futile unless there is a religious reformation, and man in Christ becomes capable of self-government.

---

[2] Marshall Berman, "Sympathy for the Devil: Faust, the '60s and the Tragedy of Development," in *American Review*, no. 19, January, 1974. New York, N.Y.: Bantam Books, 1974.

Chapter Forty-Two
The Justice of the Peace

In reading in the history of American law, I realized that, however able the histories were in recounting and analyzing major currents in court decisions, they overlooked the most common court and the most active judge of all. Prior to 1940, the major activity in the American legal system was in the hands of the local justice of the peace. This court still exists, but in many states it has been abolished.

The courts of the justices of the peace are of ancient origin. In England, the justice of the peace had as his duty to "keep the peace" in the local jurisdiction for which he was appointed. He was someone from the area, at one time from the landed gentry, and the cases he tried were not of great financial consequences and yet were important in maintaining law and order within the community.

The basic duty of the justice of the peace was, and is, the enforcement of all laws, ordinances, and statutes to maintain law and order, and to enforce peace and harmony among the people. English law made the local mayor *ex officio* a justice during this term of office, gave him precedence over all justices in the borough, and he could take the chair at any meeting, although there were and are limitations on the scope of his precedence.

In the United States, the J.P., or justice of the peace, is normally elected. His is the lowest of all the state courts, and normally he is not a lawyer. There are limits on the value of civil suits, and, in criminal cases, misdemeanors, the guilty party is not jailed unless he refused to pay the fine.

At one time, the justice of the peace court was in the United States the busiest of all courts. It once had the key role in American legal life, and some justices of the peace, whether for good or ill, were the law in their areas in the early history of the West.

The justice of the peace, not being a trained lawyer, might have few law books or none at all. He relied on the Bible, local standards, and "common sense." His decisions had to meet the demands of the local community for law and order. The decisions of the justice of the peace had, normally, great receptivity in the local community, and the courts functioned for generations with success. As legal education of an academic character increased, the standing of the justice of the peace decreased in the eyes of legislators, who were increasingly lawyers. The result was the decline, and, in some states, the elimination of the justice of the peace.

Since writing *Institutes of Biblical Law*, I have occasionally heard from justices of the peace thanking me for providing them with a convenient manual on the subject. The work is also used by them in their decisions.

What is important in all this is that we once had quite generally a means of handling most cases on the local level. Given the more Christian character and standards of earlier America, serious crimes like murder were less common, and most cases were within the jurisdiction of the justice of the peace. Within my own life-time, most superior court judges were elderly men. Many were partners in major law firms which ran for office an older member as a public service. It was a position which did not pay well, but the work then was light. The judge would step aside if his firm were involved in a case. As a partner in the firm, he sometimes still had an income. Since then, judgeships have become political rewards, and state superior courts are more crowded. The power and jurisdiction of federal courts have also grown.

Instead of a neighbor enforcing basic law, now the law system is remote to the people and to their faith. It has been federalized in the name of democracy, which has come to be another name for the centralization of powers.

A return to the justice of the peace will not solve our problems, however. The growing decay of character has created a need for courts to try cases beyond the scope of the J.P. and his court. Murder, rape, arson, and all the multitude of current offenses require more involved trials and courts of record.

The solution must begin with a return to the most basic form of localism, a stress on the faith and character of the people. Because of antinomianism, the erosion of the people's morality has been great, and no system of civil government can restore it. There must be a return to the centrality of faith and morality; nothing else will suffice.

The justice of the peace is related to the Biblical (and English, and American) hundreds courts, to the emphasis on rule in God's way and with God's law.

Chapter Forty-Three
"Remember"

Modern thinking, which has deep roots in Hellenic, medieval scholastic, and Enlightenment thinking, is strongly prone to abstractionism and intellectualism. It seeks to separate ideas and concepts from life, whereas Biblical thinking is concrete and specific.

A. G. Hebert called attention to this in its implications for the meaning of "remember." When, for example, Joshua 1:13 tells us, "Remember the word which Moses the servant of the LORD commanded you," or Malachi 4:4, "Remember ye the law of Moses my servant," Hebert points out that "the meaning is that they must obey it."[1] We cannot think like moderns and act like Christians. Memory must be linked to action.

This is very different from our view of *memory* as an English-speaking people. We identify memory with *recollection*. We can say, "I remember the first time I saw the state capitol," and it implies no action. In this sense, memory is *recall*, bringing up recollections of things past. A person with a good memory is one who had the ability to recall things from the past, knowledge acquired over the years, and so on and on. Our view of memory is past-oriented. On the other hand, the Biblical usage to which Herbert called attention is clearly present and future-oriented.

These two perspectives radically alter our Christian stance. In evangelical circles, much stress is placed on remembering one's conversion experience, the date, place, and so on. It is seen as an *experience*, not as a *call*. A *call* is to action and service, to a relationship to the present and future, whereas an *experience* is past history. If the experiential man looks to the future, it is commonly to look forward to being raptured out of this world. The called man looks to conquering the world for Christ.

If one's perspective is governed by the fact of Christ's calling, then one's memory is not a miscellaneous collection of random items but a well-marshalled perspective on the future. The past and the present are steps to God's future.

Memory is, like history, an organization of time, and the memory of too many people is simply a directionless catch-all of items. One of the impressive facts about the effective Christian men over the generations has been their focus on God's future. One of the great men of the past two centuries was General Booth, founder of the Salvation Army. One need not agree with his theology to recognize his greatness. His accomplishments were great because his focus was so totally on Jesus Christ and what He requires of us. The poet, Vachel Lindsay,

---

[1]. A. G. Hebert, "Memory...," in Alan Richardson, editor: *A Theological Word Book of the Bible* (New York, N.Y.: Macmillan, (1950) 1960), p. 143.

caught the spirit of that calling in his great poem, "General William Booth Enters Heaven."

A godly memory, in the Biblical sense as pointed out by Hebert, is very much needed by all of us. When our Lord at the Last Supper said, "Do this in remembrance of me" (1 Cor. 11:24f.), He was not summoning them simply to a faithful recall of the event but to a life of power in His service. As He had sacrificed Himself to make atonement for His people, they were to bring all things into obedience to Him in His living, continuing power. It was not simply a memorial service but a mandate for action. Christ's passover had as its forerunner Israel's passover, which began with a requirement for obedience, and then a summons to move forward and to conquer the Promised Land.

Chapter Forty-Four
God and Morality

Henry Banford Parkes, in *The Divine Order, Western Culture in the Middle Ages and the Renaissance* (1969), makes an excellent observation on a comment by Othello in Shakespeare's *Othello*. "When Othello becomes convinced of Desdemona's violation of her marriage vows, he immediately sees this as a threat to all ordered society." Othello exclaims,

> "Chaos has come again."...We may suppose that Shakespeare was not fully aware of the implicity of Othello's remarks, but the wording makes it inescapably plain that an act of unchastity meant a denial of the whole social order.[1]

Intellectually, this belief is virtually gone. Emotionally, it still is very strong among betrayed men and women.

It is curious to find that the reverse opinion is so prevalent, namely, that adultery represents freedom and pleasure, a step outside the world of order and responsibility into a realm of exemption from the necessities and burdens of order. Too often the adulterer or adulteress chooses an inferior person simply because the relationship is supposedly divorced from all burdens and responsibilities, from mature consequences. The appeal is its sin more than sex because their sexual opportunities in marriage were and are not limited. It was and is the burden of a constantly responsible relationship that they sought and seek escape from — to be young again means for them freedom from responsibility.

Responsibility means something very different from chaos. Chaos means no consequences, a world without order, hence without aging and judgment. With the rise of Romanticism, both childhood and sin have been seen as a part of a realm outside of responsibility and hence highly desired.

An important figure in this contempt is Matthew Arnold (1822-1888), a literary figure given often an undue importance because of his ideas. Full of self-pity, Arnold, like all the Romantics, is a key figure in the development of victimhood. His poem, "Dover Beach," is revealing. For Arnold, "The Sea of Faith" was at low tide. The implication of this use of tides as a figure is that faith, for Arnold, Christianity, can again be at high tide. Intellectual currents, were, for Arnold, all important. It was not an age of theology; instead what had come in was "the eternal note of readiness," and Arnold was full of self-pity.

Arnold's answer was one fully in tune with the Victorian era: morality replaced theology. God might be now scientifically untenable as a hypothesis, but morality seemed to divide the races and the nations. National power and

---

[1.] Henry Banford Parkes, *The Divine Order, Western Culture in the Middle Ages and the Renaissance* (New York, N.Y.: Alfred A. Knopf, 1969), p. 398n.

excellence came with morality, and the advanced nations were above "the lesser breeds without the law," to use Kipling's phrase, because of their moral law.

This shift from theology to morality helps explain an interesting fact. The rise of the Salvation Army led to much hostility. Some early Salvation Army members were not only mobbed but killed. But the Salvation Army met with the approval in a number of countries, of local royalty and intellectuals, who sought to further the shift from theology to morality in so doing. The Salvation Army, was, after all, famous for its good works.

The Victorian Age did believe in morality even when it failed to observe it. The eternal order had shifted from theology to morality. But, in its very origins, Romanticism had also abandoned morality, the Marquis de Sade in particular. The element of perversity quickly appeared in Romantic literature.

Most, however, replaced theology with a belief in the absoluteness of morality. Morality, however, is an aspect of theology. God as the Creator has given a necessary moral order to all creation. Moral order is an aspect of theological order, and it soon erodes without it. In belief this means no God, no morality. Without God, every man is his own source of law and morality.

With this in mind, we can better understand Othello's comment, "Chaos has come again," or, in Parkes' words, "an act of unchastity meant a denial of the whole social order." The Victorians who like Arnold substituted the moral law for God were soon succeeded by Victorians who ridiculed "the middle class," meaning Christian and evangelical, and its pre-occupation with morality and sin. Morality for them was no longer associated with God, but neither was it a part of personal behavior. The state had replaced God, and the English philosophers of idealism were radically statist. The moral realm was now the social and statist realm. It was this era that gave rise to the social gospel. Since, then, the moral issues have become socialistic ones, environmental causes, and so and so on. Morality is now socially defined, not theologically.

Instead of having reference to a cosmic supernatural order, to God, morality is now identified in terms of the natural order, Mother Earth, or Gaia. But this creates a problem. A valid and legitimate order rests on an accepted belief in ultimacy, an ultimate power and law. The vicious disorder in the Renaissance Italian city states was due to an absence of valid law and power. Torture had been common to the late Roman Empire. Its legitimacy was denied by Christendom, and it was slowly abolished, only to return full force with the Renaissance. Since 1914, and especially since 1949, it has again returned to the Western world because the legitimacy of God's law has been questioned.

The question of legitimacy and law was never solved by Islam, and, over the centuries, power has been maintained by brute force, so that terrorism has been basic to those in power and those out of power. Europe, in the late Middle Ages, by turning from Biblical to Roman premises, created centralized and autocratic regimes also. In England, the Tudor break with Rome had deeper roots than are normally recognized. The Tudors had no standing army; they were monetarily inept and foolish; they had no large bureaucracy, and they were dependent on local officials. They did have, however, a strong basis of popular support, whether we like it or not.

It is significant that, whereas medieval art sought to depict God's order, Renaissance art began the long shift from God's order to nature as the subject of art. A new priority was being revealed. Not the Last Judgment but the royal will came to be stressed, and this culminated in a depiction finally of Louis XIV as the god Zeus. The artists were now the new seers, and financial support that once went to monks shifted to the new prophets, the artists. Romanticism very clearly made the artist the source of man's new revelations, whatever they were. In Walt Whitman, this view of the artist as prophet-savior was clearly expressed.

But where was the law? For Walt Whitman, it seemed to be a mindless affirmation of democracy, free sexuality, especially for homosexuals, and not much more than the pious gushing of humanistic platitudes.

Instead of "chaos is come again," to cite again Othello's words, for too many moderns the conclusion was, "freedom is come again." The liberation of man was accomplished by the abandonment of God's law. But the prisonhouse that was closing about Wordsworth's new and "free" mankind was the prison of humanism, totalitarianism, amoral, and lawless.

The appeal to a basic order is inescapable in a fallen world. It can be to a future order, such as the Great Society, a humanistic goal which gives us the glorified City of Man, or it can be to a God-ordained order, the City of God. However much humanism proclaims an acceptance of nature, it cannot rest content with nature as it is. It seeks to conserve or to improve on it, to restore it or to protect it, but it is critical in some sense. The status quo is never enough. But from whence the norm? Ultimately, this becomes for most a personal judgment. "Science" or evolutionary hypotheses supply many norms, and there is no common assent, nor a given text, such as the Bible.

But we are assured that chaos will indeed come in again if we do not heed the messages of our humanist saviors. They who have despised Biblical morality have given to us via the modern state new laws, going into tens of thousands of volumes, whereby man is to be saved, and there is still no end to these salvationist laws. These laws are unread even by those who pass them, for who can read over 2,000 pages of often contradictory statements, and they are unreadable. They speak more of chaos than of order.

Chapter Forty-Five
Arrogant False Witness

According to the Ten Commandments, "Thou shalt not bear false witness against thy neighbour" (Ex. 20:16; Deut. 5:20). The primary reference is to courts of law and testimony therein. In courts, an oath was required of all witnesses, i.e., an oath invoking the judgment of God for false testimony. The framers of the U.S. Constitution held strongly to the necessity of an oath based on faith in the God of Scripture, "otherwise there would be nothing to bind his conscience on."[1] For many years, courts could reject the testimony of an atheist or agnostic on the grounds that he could not validly take an oath, or, if allowing the testimony, warned the jury that the man's testimony could not be backed by an oath.

This commandment also calls for honest speech among men. What can false witness include? It does require honesty. To cite an example, among one people, a child of five can ask to be included in a game played by children of ten and twelve years. He cannot play the game, but his request is never denied, with the result that the game breaks up. False witness is made to the child of five, namely, that he can compete in a game with older children.

Another example: years ago, I came to know somewhat a dying boy genius, whose heart finally gave out in his teens. As a child, the family, with reason, expected great things from him. Their pity, when his bad heart ended even his schooling very early, was great. The boy's abilities were versatile. At chess he could defeat very able men. But pity led the family to indulge the boy's whims and tantrums, and, from a happy boy he went on to become a problem and a burden. The family had borne false witness to their son.

Such instances of false witness are many, and in diverse spheres. For example, in the 1996 presidential campaign, one speaker was sharply condemned for racism because of a reference to "Chinamen" rather than Chinese. There was no ill will on his part. At one time, "Chinaman" was as correct as "Englishman" is now; in some parts of the United States, similar older usages still prevail. Was it not false witness to level unwarranted charges against the man?

Another example: A black mother filed a complaint with a Stockton, California, school district because a widely used and respected older novel referred to "African-Americans" as "darkies." Investigations soon followed.[2]

Such incidents are commonplace. In the Friday, November 29, 1996, *Record*, the vice-president of the Associated Students of the University of the Pacific,

---

[1.] Cited from George Bancroft, *History of the United States of America*, vol. 6 (1891), p. 420, by Mark A. Beliles and Stephen K. McDowell, *America's Providential History* (Charlottesville, Virginia: Providence Foundation, (1989) 1996), p. 179.

[2.] Tamma Adamek, "Novel to Stay for Now," in *The Record*, November 27, 1996, Wednesday, B1, 3.

Stockton, California, wrote an in-house memo meant to stimulate discussion. With all kinds of racial organizations on campus, why not one to focus on "the American-Caucasian race" and their culture and achievements? He was at once the target of hostile comments and criticisms by the self-styled voices of the 43 percent of the university's students. They receive 82 percent of the club funding from student activity fees.[3]

False witness exists in such incidents in many ways. Not all "minority" students agree with the stands taken by groups acting in their name. Some are greatly embarrassed by the bigotry they see manifested in such episodes.

But, across the spectrum, we see a variety of self-appointed spokesmen speaking for a particular class or race, for women or for men, for "sexual minorities," and so on and on. One is reminded of the incident in 17th century England when three (or five?) tailors issued a proclamation which began, "We, the people of England...." Such arrogance is routine now, and it is false witness and should be called so.

Routinely, churchmen speak as though they are the voice of all the people when the people are ignorant of what is said in their name. It is possible and also mandatory to speak in the name of the Lord when we speak in absolute fidelity to His word. We can and must say, "Thus saith the Lord, 'Thou shalt have none other gods before me.'" (Deut. 5:7). It is a sin not to say so when the occasion requires it. But where does God speak about a minimum wage law, or about subsidized housing?

Who speaks for me? And, whom do I speak for? How is it that, in an "age of democracy," we have more demagogues than ever all claiming to speak for more and more of us? Democracy has led too many to over-weight numbers and under-weight truth. Is it that where numbers win elections numbers over-rule truth?

Clearly, perjury is less and less a subject of legal penalty, and perjury has become routine in courts of law. Where God and His word are no longer primary in a society, there is a shift to pragmatic and man-centered considerations. Then too Pilate's old scepticism again comes to the fore: "What is truth?" (John 18:38).

A society begins and ends in false witness if its cornerstone is not Christ. Its focus apart from Christ is on man, so that it begins with a premise that is false.

Most peoples, races, and nationalities are today too prone to self-pity and to demanding a favored place in the sun. Each sees itself as a kind of church, a holy vessel before which history should kneel and give reverence. "None other gods" is foundational to the Ten Commandments because, apart from that premise, we falsify all things, and not only our words but we ourselves become false to the

---

[3.] B. D. Spence, "Race-pride memo raises debate at UOP," *The Record*, Friday November 29, 1996, p. A1, 14.

core. The sad absurdities of the two Stockton episodes cited above are no worse than what we all exhibit constantly when our lives are not God-centered, for then false witness is basic to our nature.

Chapter Forty-Six
Teleology and Law

The word and the concept of *teleology* are so alien now that a definition is necessary. Teleology is the study of meaning and design in nature; it holds that ends are immanent in nature; things move towards a given end or purpose which is pre-ordained. In the 1930s, belief in God-given teleology was much ridiculed; now it is rarely mentioned. The only teleology which is now acceptable, although not so called, is humanistic and Marxist. For humanism, man creates the goals, and man makes them come to pass, by his planning and controls. For Marxism, nature works inexorably to achieve the goal of communism, but why a blind and dead natural order should do so we are never told.

Law by its very nature is teleological, because it posits a certain order and penalizes all deviations from it. However, the cynicism concerning teleology is so great that we hear too little about the goal and purpose of law.

The Christian view of law is teleological because its view of God is providential. Romans 8:28 sums this up by declaring that God makes all things work together for good for His elect people. All peoples also are under the law of God, and hence they must all be treated as our neighbor (Lev. 19:18, 33f.). The law therefore must be free of any respect of persons, rich or poor, a fellow covenant member or an alien (Deut. 1:16-18).

This belief became deeply entrenched in Christian thinking. *All men* were seen as neighbors, and all as equally accountable. Thus, medieval man saw King Arthur as a contemporary, depicting a man of the fifth or sixth century as a twelfth century knight and ruler. There is reason to believe this was deliberate. The differences between areas no more than fifty miles apart was very great, even to their language. The English of London, or the French of Paris, was not always understandable at fifty or one hundred miles distance. Latin was for the literate truly an international language. Why then was there no attempt at "authentic" depictions of King Arthur and his "knights"? What was truly authentic for the twelfth century narrators was the equal validity of the law of God for King Arthur and for themselves. This made them contemporaries. In this respect, they were more internationally minded than the people of the twentieth century, who are sharply aware of ethnic and cultural differences.

With the age of exploration, some men brought back to Europe wives from Africa and Asia, and this was no problem where the women became Christians. The explorers were both far harsher and far more tolerant than our moderns, because they saw these foreign peoples not as primitives, but as their contemporaries. Their differences were seen as essentially religious, not as differing stages of evolution. A once common Christian expression, now rarely heard, was applied to any man of a lower moral status: "There but for the grace of God go I."

Because law points to a desired state, it is theological and teleological. The "theology" can vary, but the fact of a goal remains. To say "Thou shalt not kill," and, "Thou shalt not commit adultery," is to look to a murder-free and adultery-free world. To say, "Thou shalt not steal," is to work towards a world order in which other people's properties are respected. A world order without the sins and crimes enumerated by the law is thus the desired world and the goal of the law.

In recent generations, some "minority" groups in the United States and elsewhere have at times been treated indulgently in their "minor" lawlessness because they are held to be incapable of behaving differently. This is a form of racism and a disrespect for the law.

One of the aspects of American behavior that has been commendable, as against the form of racism just cited, has been an insistence in many quarters on a like standard for all. Thus, an immigrant, understanding very little English, erred because he misunderstood his instructions. He was bluntly rebuked and told that one of his duties on the job was to understand what he was told, and to ask if he failed to do so, or get fired.

The twelfth century writer on King Arthur was more accurate than the twentieth century writers on American Puritans who can be painstaking in their research on clothing and customs while projecting their bigotry on a people they refuse to understand.

Teleology is inescapable, and, if we reject the Biblical form thereof, we will become victims of alien teleologies, especially humanistic and Marxist ones. Of late, Islamic teleologies have become increasingly prevalent.

Chapter Forty-Seven
The Last Judgment

The law points to a judge and to judgment. Commandments and laws are not given into the void. They presuppose a place of settlement, an accounting, so that wrongs can be righted and restitution and reformation made. Laws cannot be separated from courts of law nor from judgment.

This is true of history. It is the arena of law, and its court and its time of judgment are the conclusion of history. Our Lord, in Matthew 25:31-46, speaks of the Last Judgment as a time when all accounts are settled and the reality of men's lives are revealed as against the appearances.

Over the centuries, the Last Judgment has often had a prominent place in the life of the church. The Last Judgment concludes all history. It is the witness to the triumph of Christ over all His enemies. Before the end, He reigns through His saints, by whom all things are put under His feet (1 Cor. 15:25). Then, with the Last Judgment, the law enforces the totality of God's justice to reward the righteous and to punish the unjust.

The Last Judgment has thus been a witness over the centuries to the coming triumph of absolute justice. The Judge for the Trinity will be Jesus Christ (Acts 17:31), who will judge the world "in righteousness," in justice. All shall stand before His judgment seat (Rom. 14:9-10). God "hath given him authority to execute judgment also, because he is the Son of Man" (John 5:27). He is the righteous Judge (2 Tim. 4:8).

The Last Judgment is God's final judging of mankind by His law. He is the Judge in the final court because it is His law that has been broken.

As H. B. Clark wrote,

> Christian law recognizes the truth of the ancient proverb that "As he (a man) thinks in his heart, so is he" (Prov. 23:7) — in other words, that transgressions arise not out of the environment, in which one finds himself, but out of the human mind or heart. In respect of this doctrine, Jesus said that "...from within, out of the heart of men, proceed evil thoughts, adulteries, fornications, murders, thefts, covetousness, wickedness, deceit, lasciviousness, an evil eye, blasphemy, pride, foolishness. All these evil things come from within, and defile the man." (Mk. 7:21-23)
>
> Therefore the law is concerned with respect to the mental and spiritual condition of the individual who, as the blind Pharisee, should "cleanse first that which is within — that the outside...may be clean also."[1]

The Last Judgment means that all history's wrongs are righted, and all injustice wiped out. The conclusion of history demonstrates that only God is

---

[1] H. B. Clark: *Biblical Law* (Portland, Oregon: Binsfords & Mort, (1943); second edition, 1944), para. 20, p. 11.

God, that man's attempt to be his own god and law is doomed to defeat and to total repudiation before the end.

The Last Judgment is also the link between time and eternity. Despite the very great difference between time and eternity, they are still connected. Because sin and death are alike destroyed, and because perfect justice prevails, eternity becomes the place of fulfillment. In Revelation 22:1-4 we are given an insight into that new creation. The "river of the water of life" flows from "the throne of God and of the Lamb." Then we have a symbol that defies literal understanding. "The tree of life" is "in the midst of the street" and yet "on either side of the river." Christ, "the Lamb," is on the throne, but He is also the river of life and the tree of life. The tree bears "twelve" kinds of fruit, i.e., the fulness of fruits, continually, "and the leaves of the tree were for the healing of the nations." Potentiality and actuality are one. In the new creation, sin no longer intervenes with its offer of a false potentiality, to be as God (Gen. 3:5), so that the fruit of the tree now enables us in our creaturely estate, to realize our potentialities in an eternal actuality, as K. Schilder has pointed out.

Because the curse is gone, there is now full and perfect service. Men are now eternally what they have made themselves to be (Rev. 22:11, 15).

In Greco-Roman culture, work was for slaves, not for a free people. St. Paul, however, in 2 Thessalonians 3:10 held that, if any will not work, let him not eat. Instead of being punishment, work was for Christians the means of reclaiming this fallen world for God. It is easy enough to find exceptions to this in Christendom, but Christianity faced paganism and pagan attitudes toward work on all sides, and it took time to change them. "Western civilization" only became possible because a considerable change did occur.

Prior to World War II, a constant theme of song and sermon in the church was, "Work, for the night is coming when man's work is done." The subject was approached from every perspective and strongly stressed.

The Last Judgment points to the righting of all accounts and to the perfection of justice. Apart from this doctrine, law loses its importance, and pessimism deepens in a culture. The proclamation of the doctrine of the Last Judgment is thus an affirmation of law, justice, and hope. The absence of this faith is devastating to any culture. It is not at all surprising that, as antinomianism has prevailed, the meaning of the Last Judgment has eroded and waned.

Chapter Forty-Eight
The State and the Last Judgment

The Last Judgment is God's culminating and final act of justice; it is the righting of all wrongs and the cleansing of history from all its sins and evils.

The state, according to Romans 13:1ff., is God's ministry of justice, or should be. But civil rulers and officials are born in *original sin*, alien to God, and quickly fall into *actual sin*. They cannot, as the medieval church, and Wyclif, held, therefore be justly lords over anything. This does not justify revolution but it does incur God's judgment. According to Sir. R. W. Carlyle and A. J. Carlyle, Egidius Colona's views could be summarized thus:

> It is only when the Church delivers him [the ruler] from original sin by regeneration and from actual sin by absolution that he can become the just lord of his property, and it is right that this property should be under the Church from whom he holds his lordship.[1]

Protestants would substitute "under God" for "under the Church," but otherwise, Reformed thinkers would agree. "The only true authority is a just authority," or, as we might also say, "Justice is the end or purpose of the State,"[2] and "law is the embodiment of justice."[3] From this perspective, the state has a Christian moral and theological purpose. The modern state has a like purpose, but with this difference: it has substituted itself for God. The modern state sees itself as the maker and definer of law and morality, and the U. S. Supreme Court recognizes no judge above or beyond itself.

Men like John Salisbury saw the ruler as representing the image of God when just, but the image of wickedness when tyrants. "The origin of tyranny is iniquity" and the source of all the world's troubles and evils.[4] "The authority of the king is the authority of law [or right], not of wrong....[T]he authority of wrong belongs to the devil, and not to God, and the king is the servant of him whose work he does."[5] The law makes the ruler, not the ruler the law. "Where there is no law there is no authority." In terms of a famous phrase of Bracton, "There is NO king where will rules and not law."[6] This means that no authority can legitimately make laws which are contrary to the law of God.[7]

---

[1] Sir R. W. Carlyle and A. J. Carlyle: *A History of the Medieval Political Theory in the West,* vol. V, *The Political Theory of the Thirteenth Century* (Edinburgh, Scotland: William Blackwood & Sons, 1928), p. 407f.

[2] *ibid.,* V, p. 458.

[3] *ibid.,* V, p. 462.

[4] *ibid.,* vol. III, *Political Theory from the Tenth Century to the Thirteenth,* by A.J. Carlyle, p. 138.

[5] *ibid.,* V, p. 35.

[6] *ibid.,* V, p. 38.

[7] *ibid.,* vol. II, *The Political Theory of the Roman Lawyers and the Canonists, from the Tenth Century to the Thirteenth Century,* p. 228.

St. Augustine, in *The City of God*, held that rulers without the Biblical God are not more than bands of robbers exploiting the people. A like opinion is cited by A. J. Carlyle:

> And Sedulius Scotus, warning evil rulers of the ruin which impends over them, of the judgment of God which awaits them both in this world and the next, exclaims: "What are impious kings but the greatest robbers of the earth, fierce as lions, ravening like wolves; but they are great today and perish tomorrow, and of them God has said, 'They reigned, but not by Me'; they arose as princes, but I knew them not." The evil ruler or tyrant is no true king; he is only, as Cicero indeed had called him, a wild beast, the most terrible and loathsome known to the world.[8]

The modern state has no transcendental source of validation. It derives its power from the people and yet pretends to a justice beyond the people. *Democracy* somehow possesses, a la Rousseau, a will, the general will, that transcends the people. In practice, there is no truth nor justice beyond the will of the state.

To identify the temporal with the eternal is to identify what belongs to a fallen world with God, not simply as a servant but as his manifest presence. Thus, when in 1492 Rodrigo Borgia was elected pope, Rome celebrated by comparing him to Alexander the Great and Caesar. One banner declared, "Rome was great under Caesar. Now she is even greater. Caesar was a man. Alexander is a God!"[9] Rome became the center of evil, of debauchery, homosexuality, syphilis, and ugly cynicism.[10] One prominent observer, calling attention to the papal palace as the scene of rape, incest, and the abuse of adolescent boys and girls, held that the time of the Antichrist had come.[11]

What happened in papal Rome was surpassed by the Renaissance tyrants. In the 20th century especially, the Renaissance has been held to be, not an age of horror and tyranny as it was, but a time of greatness because of the revival of paganism. The legacy of the Renaissance tyrants has been the prized heritage of the humanists of the 20th century. Without transcendence, the modern state has become god walking on earth.

In the latter half of the 20th century, the difference in the concepts of justice, Biblical and humanistic, have come into focus. In Scripture, justice is defined by God and is set forth in His law. For the modern state, justice is defined by man and is expressed in humanistic laws and regulations. An example of this is *affirmative action*, the legal efforts by the states and the federal government to compensate for past discriminations against minority groups by discriminating in their favor. This has led to new injustices.[12]

---

8. *ibid.*, I, *The Second Century to the Ninth*, by A. J. Carlyle, p. 228.

9. Ivan Cloulas, *The Borgias* (New York, N.Y.: Franklin Watts, (1987) 1989), p. 70.

10. *ibid.*, pp. 137ff.

11. *ibid.*, p. 221.

12. See James W. Wilson, "The case for ending racial preferences," in *U.S. News & World Report*, December 23, 1996, vol. 121, no. 25, p. 31f.

It is true that at times affirmative action has helped people singly.[13] It has, however, done this at the price of injustice to others. People have qualified as fire fighters and police officers because of race rather than ability. Injustice is corrected by injustice.

This is a consequence of the premise of humanistic justice, the satisfaction of man's will rather than God's word. The basic premise of God's justice is no respect of persons in judgment (Deut. 1:16-18). It is God's justice that must prevail, not human factors and considerations. The respect of persons, with the best of intentions, still leads to the warping of justice and the tearing of society's fabric, whoever does it.

This does *not* mean that God's justice has no regard for the person. The great parable of the Last Judgment (Matt. 25:31-46) tells us that Jesus Christ holds His people, or those who profess to be His people, to a very clear requirement: "Inasmuch as ye did it not to one of the least of these, ye did it not to me" (Matt. 25:45). God's law, not man's humanistic wishes, is the test. True justice is defined by God's law, not man's will. At the Last Judgment, the nations themselves shall be judged (Matt. 25:32).

[13.] See Debra Dickerson, "The martial melting pot," in *U.S. News & World Report*, December 23, 1996, vol. 121, no. 25, pp. 32-34.

Chapter Forty-Nine
Law and Polytheism

Clark Kerr of the University of California lectured some years ago on the need to recognize that the multiversity has replaced the university. The presupposition of the university is Christian in that it is assumed that, because there is one God, there is a common universe of truth, law, and meaning. If, however, we have a multiverse, many systems separately evolving out of nothing, there is no common origin and meaning.

The implications of this, while seldom stated explicitly are revolutionary. Without the Biblical God, there is no common meaning, and truth is as diverse as the multiverse. There is then no common morality, only a variety of values which are optional because no common over-all truth exists. There is then no absolute good and evil, no absolute truth. Every man has thus the option of choosing his own truth and his own values.

If truth and meaning are universal, then all men must recognize the truth or pay the consequences of being in sin or error and thereby having reality against them. We can compare this to gravity: if we have the universal sway of gravity, then to disbelieve in gravity is potentially dangerous. Similarly, if the Biblical God is indeed what and whom He declares Himself to be, there can be no reality nor life apart from Him without disaster.

If we have a multiverse, there is then no common ground, and a commonality can only be established by imperialism. The decline of Christian thinking has seen the rise of imperialism, the newest form of which is one-worldism. If men lack a God-given commonality, meaning, and truth, only by coercion can they be brought within a common fold or flock.

There is no universal truth nor necessity in a polytheistic scheme of things, and the idea of a multiverse is simply a revival of polytheism. It is noteworthy that the Death of God school of theology of the late 1960s and early 1970s espoused polytheism. As Hamilton noted, "Now any child of Moses or Calvin will know why he cannot greet polytheism with unambiguous applause: when everything is divinized, nothing can be shaped or altered."[1] As Hamilton observed, David Hume, in *The Natural History of Religion*, saw that monotheism makes rational understanding possible and sees truth as possible, but he favored it as leading to courage rather than self-abasement, and doubt rather than willful certainty.[2]

It does lead to problems, however. With polytheism there is a loss of future because no ordained good can mark our tomorrows. The future is as bleak as the past because no truth nor good is the assured objective of history.

---

[1] William Hamilton: *On Taking God out of the Dictionary* (New York, N.Y.: McGraw-Hill Book Co., 1974), p. 217.

[2] *ibid.*, p. 218.

Ostensibly, polytheism provides for freedom, but this means little when meaning is denied to all things. Under polytheism, definition is eroded because there is no common and universal meaning so that freedom becomes meaningless. Men then live in an Orwellian world where freedom can mean slavery, and peace can mean perpetual war.

Law then becomes the will of the state and no more. In the 20th century, the U. S. Supreme Court, having severed law from God, has become itself the determiner of law. Its concern thereby shifts from *justice* to a polytheistic doctrine of *law*, law as the will of the state and of the court. Law is thereby separated from objective truth and from God's definition of good and evil. When Pilate said, "What is truth?" (John 18:38), he in effect said, "What is the law?", and he rendered a pragmatic decision to please the people and to safeguard his career.

One of the many problems with polytheism is that it does not confine itself to universities (or multiversities), nor to judges and scholars. It quickly becomes common property, and the result is as in the time of the judges: "In these days there was no king in Israel: every man did that which was right in his own eyes" (Judges 21:25). "No king" meant that God was not their king (1 Sam. 8:7). Moral anarchy led to slavery.

One of the absurdities of our time is the common and intense protest by moral relativists against laws they dislike. In spite of their polytheistic faith in many gods and many truths, such people tend to demand instinctively their version of truth imperialistically! Lacking confidence in its inevitability, they must move imperialistically to force their version of truth onto others.

For the Christian, Jesus Christ is the truth (John 14:6). Truth is an aspect of God's being. He is the God of truth (Ps. 31:5; Lev. 10:10, marginal reading), and His truth is everlasting because He is everlasting (Ps. 100:5; 146:6). Our English *amen* comes from *aman*, to confirm, stand firm, trust. To conclude prayers with *amen*, meaning true, reliable, is to affirm that we pray in trust to an unchanging and eternally true God; He does not change (Mal. 3:6).

Because God is the God of truth, He demands truth of men (Deut. 5:20). Because He is truth, man and his society must be founded on truth. Truth is God's righteousness, His justice, His law; it is a moral and religious fact. In the modern view, "academic freedom" means freedom from responsibility, whereas in the Biblical usage freedom is freedom from sin to follow righteousness or justice. The Holy Spirit is identified with truth (John 16:13), and He leads men into the fullness of truth. In John 14:6, Jesus Christ identifies life and truth with Himself, and He is the only way of life. God's word is truth (John 17:17) because He is truth.

The separation of law from God, from truth, has been the death of law, which has given way to bureaucratic regulations, most of all in the Marxist states. We can thus say, no God, no law, only tyranny and death for man and society.

Chapter Fifty
"The Sanctity of the Sovereign"

When I was very young, a toddler learning to walk, I often lost my balance and fell. The fact that I was ignorant of the law of gravity did not prevent me from falling. This fact is important in our Kantian-Hegelian world. The presuppositions of modern philosophy are that the real world is the world conceived by the mind of the philosopher and intellectual whose reason ascertains its own reality because the rational is the real. As a result, persons who have never heard of Kant or Hegel will tell you what reality is because they so conceive it. Their "wisdom" is introduced with the decisive, "Well, I think...." Theirs is the new voice from a new Mt. Sinai.

Our age cannot be understood apart from this presupposition. Jesus Christ said, as God incarnate, "I am the...truth" (John 14:6). Modern man says, if truth there be, I am the truth.

An old expression, once common, now less used but still operative, is "the sanctity of the sovereign." Charles Norris Cochrane had this to say about its meaning in ancient Rome:

> The sanctity of the sovereign being taken to imply that also of his ministers, this fact served to place the whole administration above criticism. An edict of 385 forbade discussion regarding the merits of any one chosen by the emperor to serve him, pronouncing it the equivalent of sacrilege to question the imperial judgment. Entrance to public office thus became a kind of ordination; to leave it was to lay down a sacred trust. With the establishment of these principles the imperial service assumed a veritably hieratical character.[1]

Julian the Apostate carried this to its logical conclusion when he banned the setting up of private (or Christian) schools, and the licensing of all teachers was required.[2]

The term, "the sanctity of the sovereign," has less usage now, but its application is no less important. In the modern age, the king's person was so sacred that any attempt on his person led to the most vicious kind of execution. To be drawn and quartered was the punishment for anyone, as in France and England, who plotted or attempted, or killed a king. He would be dragged to the place of execution by a horse or behind a cart. Evisceration would follow, being pulled apart while alive by horses, and then his body cut up into pieces for his "sacrilege."

Whenever or wherever the sovereign is a man or an institution, the penalty has normally been savage. As modern republics slip into becoming sovereign

---

[1] Charles Norris Cochrane, *Christianity and Classical Culture* (London, England: Oxford University Press, (1940) 1977), p. 322.
[2] *ibid.*, p. 286

states, their penalties likewise grow in severity, their officials gaining immunity in the process.

Where God is the sovereign, men recognize that hell is the self-chosen penalty of all rebels, but, where civil rebels are concerned, hell must be here and now, and visible to all. The American expression, "You can't fight city hall," is early evidence of the state's claims to a right to all attempts to challenge its "right" to a freedom from accountability.

There is a serious problem with every humanistic concept of "the sanctity of the sovereign." Law is the expression of the will of the sovereign for his subjects, or, in a classic statement, "Law may be defined, 'The command of the sovereign power, containing a common rule of life for the subjects.'"[3] Non-theistic law lacks universality or catholicity. It is not "a common rule of life" because it is oriented to class interests, statist concerns, and self-serving goals that are hostile to catholicity. They serve capital or labor, farm or city, a specific race, a philosophy such as Marxism, and so on.

God's law applies to all men without distinction because all men are *under God*, whereas in humanistic societies men are *under men* with their own passionate goals. "The sanctity of the sovereign" is thereby transferred from God to some men and their civil orders. In ancient Rome, the ruler was *pontifus maximus*, combining in his person both rule and priesthood. His sanctity made him thus by law beyond criticism.

Christianity, by separating priesthood from the state, insisted, *first*, that God's law must be made the law of nations. It is significant that Biblical family law was early stressed and enforced. *Second*, whether or not the church assumed its responsibility, it was now the proclaimer of the word. Its duty was a prophetic one, to declare the word of God to kings and commoners. It is noteworthy that the English Puritans called their training sessions for the clergy *schools for prophets*. *Third*, the ruler had to submit to the sanctity of the word of God. One may disagree with some of the actions taken by men like Ambrose of Milan, but he clearly saw it as his duty to demand that the emperor be ruled by God's law, not his own. The logic of this led to the humbling of Emperor Henry IV at Canossa in the eleventh century. One may disagree with the policies of Hildebrand (Pope Gregory VII), but the premise that God's word must be above all men and rulers remains valid. *Fourth*, Christianity by separating priesthood from the state, and by holding that the primary sphere is God and heaven, has made clear that the source of all law is God, and His eternal order governs the temporal. God is the true sovereign, and His is the true realm of sanctity.

[3.] "Law," in *Encyclopedia Brittannica*, vol. II (Edinburgh, Scotland, 1971), p. 883.

Chapter Fifty-One
Presuppositions and Law

All thinking is based on presuppositions which organize and direct thought. The world of factuality gives us quintillion upon quintillion facts which are meaningless unless a premise of organization and meaning exists. Just as Euclidean geometry begins with its presuppositions, certain axioms which govern all things and provide the framework whereby a theorem can be proven, so all thinking in every field has its particular presuppositions.

The presupposition of Christian thinking is the triune God and His enscriptured word. The presupposition of humanism is the mind of man as the ultimate arbiter and judge. Our presuppositions govern our thinking. A false presupposition gives us false conclusions.

Every kind of law rests on a presupposition, so that Biblical law and humanistic law, while perhaps agreeing on a specific law, i.e., "Thou shalt not kill," means different things thereby. In Biblical law, the premise is that God, the Creator and Governor over all life, can alone decide when and where the taking of life is permissible. In humanistic law, murder may be forbidden where man decides that something should be protected. The protected life may be that of a rattlesnake, or of a mountain lion: what is protected is decided by the state in terms of environmental considerations. Where human life is concerned, God's law has a different presupposition than does the state's law. God, as the Creator, holds that He alone can govern the taking of life, whereas the state determines what is a tenable killing in terms of its interests.

Other factors also govern law. Those who believe in original sin and total depravity will, *first*, see man as a sinner who must be kept in reign by God's law. Because of his fallen nature, man has a propensity to sin, and he must be kept in check by the law and the penalties thereof. Without the restraint of the law, man will destroy society and create a world of evil and terror.

As against this, humanism sees man, not as a sinner, but either as naturally good, or, at worst, as neutral. Crime then becomes an abnormality and not the inclination of fallen man. There are variations to this, as witness the Marquis de Sade, who made crime both natural and good and insisted on its recognition as man's true way of life, the natural life.

Second, in the Christian perspective, man is a responsible creature, responsible to God, a sinner because he is in rebellion against God. Humanism sees man as a victim and therefore to some degree not responsible by virtue of insanity, a bad environment, an evil heredity, a dysfunctional family, and so on and on. Humanism thereby makes the criminal a victim.

In my childhood, a man who was regarded as great, and a major pioneer in human thought, was Judge Benjamin Barr ("Ben") Lindsey (1869-1943). Judge of the Denver, Colorado, juvenile court (1900-1927), he wrote *Problems of the*

Children (1903), *The Beast*, with Harvey O'Higgins (1910), *The Revolt of Modern Youth* with Wainwright Evans (1935), and *The Companiate Marriage*, also with Evans (1927). Judge Lindsey was hailed as a modern prophet and a major shaper of the 20th century, which he was. He was a creator of juvenile law and courts, wherein children would ostensibly be given the fair trial denied them in the adult courts.

Now courts have always been imperfect, before and after Lindsey. But Lindsey assumed a degree of innocence on the part of juvenile offenders. He was a romantic, in the school of Wordsworth in his view of children and their innocence, and he saw the legal system as derelict in their treatment. The consequence of Judge Lindsey's legal revolution was apparent by the 1990s. Juveniles, as young as six and seven years of age, were committing serious crimes. By 1970, according to a police detective in a major city, young teenagers were ready to kill a man for as little as $20. The myth of innocence had protected evil children and youth, and they had exploited the myth also of victimhood.

A legal revolution had taken place, with corrosive results. The child had come to be seen as only marginally responsible. Responsibility was placed at the door of the family, society, capitalism, heredity, and so on. A prison guard who c. 1950 worked for a time in a juvenile detention center said that these juveniles were far more dangerous than convicts; they delighted in evil, whereas veteran criminals had a more pragmatic view.

More than a change in attitude concerning juvenile crime had taken place. Adult criminals had also come to be regarded as also only marginally responsible. Earlier, under the Biblical perspective, the offense was seen as *sin*. Now, it was called a *crime*. The concept of sin presupposes a sinner, but this is no longer true of crime, because the criminal is seen as a product, not a cause, and the blame is placed on the family, society, capitalism, and other like "causes."

Social experiments in varying forms of economy and civil polity have not reduced crime, because crime has moral foundations, and morality as a cause is excluded by modern thought. Our problems, President John F. Kennedy told a university audience early in the 1960s, are now technological, not moral, ones. Under that illusion, we have gone from crisis into crisis, trying to spend our way into non-moral "solutions" that have aggravated our problems.

The Romantic movement substituted *feelings* for *moral concerns* in the confidence that its feelings represented a higher level of purity than a sin-conceived church could provide. The purity of feeling so prized by the Romantic poets has come to its fruition, in that the feelings exalted have become more and more degenerate and perverse. The results have been pornography, perversion, and wild criminality.

Presuppositions underlie all human thought, and presuppositions are inevitably religious. Because religion is the "ultimate concern," our presuppositions arise out of our ultimate concern. But the presuppositions of fallen man are evil; they are rooted and grounded in original sin, in man's desire to be his own god, knowing or determining good and evil for himself (Gen. 3:5). Thus, when fallen man becomes a lawmaker, he seeks to protect his own ultimacy, his own sin. The laws he then creates have as a given factor his respect of persons. They are highly protective of himself and his allies in sin. The more de-Christianized his system of law becomes, the more partisan and warped it becomes. In time, moral limits are replaced by pragmatism. It is interesting that Burton Hersh, in *The Old Boys, The American Elite and the Origins of the CIA* (1992), could say of the influence of a prominent homosexual in American foreign intelligence work from World War I into the 1960s, that he re-ordered the assumptions "according to which Americans did business in the world." "Ethical limits fell away."[1] Our presuppositions shape our lives and our laws.

The common dictionary definition of law is that it is "a binding custom or practice of a community: a rule of conduct or action prescribed or formally recognized as binding or enforced by a controlling authority." The neglected part of this definition is "by a controlling authority" because it raises the religious question: Who or what is the god of the legal system — man, the state, or the Biblical God? This question cannot be avoided legitimately because we then conceal our religious roots, falsify the meaning of law, and disguise the fact of our unanswered problem.

There can be no thinking, nor law, without religious presuppositions. Without such premises, we simply have a vast realm of meaningless or brute factuality. We renounce then the possibility of meaning. To do so would be consistent thinking, but it would force an honest conclusion on the humanist; he would have to admit his total bankruptcy and ignorance, and this he refuses to do.

The world of law is religious because it designates certain forms of behavior as wrong and implicitly evil, and the opposite as permitted and good. Law is inescapably religious, but not necessarily Christian. Law is always the key form of religious expression, and, in the modern world, the anti-Christian nature of the laws of nations is concealed by a denial of the religious nature of all laws.

[1.] Burton Hersh, *The Old Boys, The American Elite and the Origins of the CIA* (New York, N.Y.: Charles Scribner's Sons, 1992), p. 255.

Chapter Fifty-Two
Why Law?

A relevant question, which must be confronted, is, why law? Why should there be any law whatsoever? This question was raised by, among others, Ted Bundy, the serial killer of a number of young women. He had confessed to killing two or three dozen women, and some believed him to be guilty of the rape and murder of fifty or a hundred. Before his execution in January, 1989, "he rambled on once about hunters who stalked and killed deer and were never plagued by a guilty conscience. Why are we so moralistic, Bundy wanted to know, when it comes to human life? Why is a human life worth more than a deer's life?"[1] This is a logical question, if you do not believe in the Christian God, nor that man is made in His image. Certainly the Marquis de Sade denied that any crime existed except Christianity because he denied its God and law.

Long before that, however, others had denied the validity of any law of eternal validity, binding on all men always. The Greek gods were above the law, and great men began to share that "divine privilege." Socrates and Plato clearly held that view, and Plato's *Republic* had no laws, only philosopher-kings. The philosopher-kings controlled and regulated all others but were themselves subject to none. The result of such thinking was the rise of tyrants. Only late in life did Plato write his study of law and allow, for an interim at least, the use of law.

Like thinking prevailed in Rome. The emperors were gods in the making, and they were therefore above the dictates of law and morality. Caligula and others took this very seriously, as Suetonius reports in the *Lives of the First Twelve Caesars*. Because law was for mere mortals, gods in the making felt free to break every kind of law.

The classical heritage lingered in medieval Europe. Kings and emperors could be zealous in enforcing God's law on their subjects, but they themselves, as time passed, began to see exemption from the law as a royal privilege.

Others besides rulers laid claim to a like immunity. Both church and university saw their role as above men's judgment, and the doctrine of academic freedom (or *freedom from accountability*) is still with us. This was also basic to the concept of the divine right of kings. We see versions of this in the rationales of civil officials in their violations of God's law. When Otto Scott, in *James I*, wrote about the homosexuality of that monarch, one historian criticized him for not respecting "the royal privilege."

The most militant attack on the idea of law came from the Marquis de Sade, who held that, because he rejected God, he thereby had rejected all law. This

---

[1.] Dr. Elizabeth Loftus and Katherine Ketchum, *Witness for the Defense* (New York, N.Y.: St. Martin's Press, 1991), p. 91.

was, indeed, a logical conclusion: no God, no law. To reject the one is to reject both. This for Sade meant the freedom to rob, rape, kill, bear false witness, practice incest, homosexuality, bestiality, and more.

No God, no law, this was a logical conclusion for fallen man to take. Man's original sin, to be his own god, law-maker, and judge (Gen. 3:5) means that no over-arching law-order can exist. Man's self-will then becomes the only tenable law. With this premise, Ted Bundy's challenge to any and all laws banning the pursuit and rape-murder of young women becomes tenable. The direction on anti-Christian culture is thus a suicidal, Sadean one.

The answer to this has at times been a pragmatic one. Both Cicero and Voltaire wanted the "common man" to hang on to some kind of faith to avoid social anarchy. Exemption from law would be the privilege of the elite. They would be, in effect, the new gods, safeguarded by the myth of morality and law which bound the peoples.

But the gods who died for the Roman intellectuals were in time dead also for the "common man" as well. The gap between the top and the bottom in any society is never as great as men imagine. Moreover, these intellectuals try to substitute an insanely invalid notion of order for the reality of creation. As Charles Norris Cochrane observed,

> It is precisely at this point that the idealist commits the crime of Prometheus in seeking to appropriate what belongs to Zeus or, like Adam in the garden eats of the forbidden fruit in order to become "like God". In other words, what he does is to treat knowledge not as a means to 'wisdom' but as a source of "power". This power to which he thus aspires proves, however, to be quite illusory. For what he has in fact accomplished is to substitute his notion of order for the order which exists in the universe; the fictitious for the actual; the dead concept for the living reality. His problem is thus to give currency to the counterfeit of cosmic order by persuading or compelling men to accept it as genuine. The effort to do so constitutes the history of "politics" in classical antiquity.[2]

It is revelatory of modern man's Kantian premises that he believes that his idea of order is thereby the actual order. He affirms with Hegel that his conception of reality is reality because he is a philosopher. Post-Kantian man sees himself as *the creator* because the knowable world is the construct of his mind; it lives because he and his kind of thinker live, and it can die with them. Now, because Kantian thinking sees man as the *knower* who creates the world and its order, it sees itself also as the *executioner.* The creator-man must re-order reality as his rationalization requires.

Thus, what he wants and needs are not laws but regulations and controls. The amount of laws passed by the U.S. Congress are few when compared to all the regulations and controls issued by the federal bureaucracy. However, even the

---

[2.] Charles Norris Cochrane, *Christianity and Classical Culture* (London, England: Oxford University Press, (1940) 1977), p. 98.

ostensible laws passed by Congress are commonly regulations. Of one such "law," to further free trade supposedly, the two volume index covered many hundreds of pages. It was said that no man had read the whole "law," which was framed by many groups of "experts" and then put together. But this "law" then governed all Americans, none of whom had more than minimal knowledge of it!

God's law concerns offenses against His order. Man's law attempts to create an imaginary order and becomes a form a disorder.

Why law? Why God's law? Because there is a fundamental and given law order, ordained and created by God to bless His people and His creation, and that order must not only be protected but advanced. This means that one order, God's, is true, and all others are false. Tertullian at this point was ahead of others in the early church because he insisted that the choice was not between two truths, two sets of laws, or two commonwealths, but between right and wrong. Where the Roman state's view of order was concerned, "we have no pressing inducement to take part in your public meetings; nor is there aught more entirely foreign to us than affairs of state. We acknowledge one all-embracing commonwealth — the world."[3] For Tertullian, that world was God's, not Rome's, and God's law and word must prevail, not man's nor Rome's.

To question God's law means to accept Bundy's question, why is killing a deer morally valid, but not killing any man or woman? To deny God is to answer that question, but not validly. Babies are now routinely aborted by the millions, but, in some areas killing deer and even rattlesnakes is proscribed. If man sets the standards, there is no objective law nor morality which can protect man as against the rattlesnake. There is then no law, only controls and regulations.

[3.] Tertullian, *Apology*, no. 38, in Alexander Roberts, James Donaldson: *The Ante-Nicene Fathers* (Grand Rapids, Michigan: Eerdmans, 1980 reprint), vol. III, p. 45f.

Chapter Fifty-Three
The Dracula Solution

Dracula is better known to fiction than to history, but there actually was a Prince Dracula (1431-1476), known also as Vlad the Impaler. Born Vlad Tepes, the second son of Vlad II, Dracul, ruler of Wallachia. The Turks at that time were moving into the Balkans and conquering much of it. After a defeat, Vlad II was required to send his two younger sons, Dracul and Radu "the Handsome," as hostages of the Turks. Radu in time was successfully seduced into homosexuality by Sultan Murad II, but Dracul escaped to seize power in Wallachia in 1448. He then waged war against Turkey until his assassination in 1476. Wallachia covered an area now a part of both Romania and Hungary. During the 39 years of his rule, he is said to have killed between 40,000 and 100,000 people in an area then populated by 500,000.

Dracul, whose life was governed by an over-powering hatred of Turks, was in his methods and standards very much a Turk and a product of their training.

Dracul, or Dracula, controlled his people, and often his enemies, by total terror. When Turkish envoys on one occasion refused to remove their turbans in his throne room, he had their headgear hammered on to their heads. A fountain not usually used was equipped with a golden cup for those who wanted a drink of water; none dared steal it, knowing the extent of Dracul's punishment. Adulterous women were subjected to unspeakable tortures before execution. The Renaissance was a time of great brutality and tortures, but Dracul was in a class almost alone.[1]

To this day, in the area Dracul once ruled, he is a national hero to some, both because of his wars against the Turks, and his maintenance of law and order.

From a Christian perspective, the two ways of obtaining law and order are, on the one hand, revolution, coercion, and compulsion, and, on the other, regeneration. Without regeneration, fallen man's nature leads to lawlessness and violence. The police power of the state is a necessary *check* to man in his sin, but it cannot reform nor change man more than superficially. Whenever and wherever the state sees itself as the way to the good society it becomes of necessity coercive to attain that goal. If it moderates its methodology to favor education, it becomes progressively a more compulsory education. Regenerating people is beyond the capacity of any state; its natural recourse is to the power the state commands, coercion. The state's logical direction, when non-Christian, is to become increasingly coercive.

This does not mean that the church does not resort to the same strategy at times. Dostoyevsky's *Grand Inquisitor* is an excellent depiction of this. The goal

---

[1.] Radu Florescu and Raymond T. McNally, *Dracula, A Biography of Vlad the Impaler* (New York, N.Y.: Hawthorn Books, 1973); Raymond T. McNally and Radu Florescu, *In Search of Dracula* (New York, N.Y.: Warner (1972) 1973).

is to *compel* men to be good and to give them no other choice. The choice then, as Dostoyevsky saw, is slavery, not freedom.

The more the state separates itself from Christianity the more it resorts to coercion, and its gospel of a true world order is one of slavery. The problem is compounded when both church and state see coercion as the solution.

When Dracul placed a golden cup at an isolated water fountain, no man dared steal it because Dracul's murderous wrath could wipe out the city and reach far into the countryside. The people of Wallachia were not made more truly moral by Dracul but only more cowed.

Under Joseph Stalin, some Russians believed life to be safer because of the fear of Stalin. Since then, some have longed for the security of the Stalin and Brezhnev years. Slavery does offer a security that freedom does not, but it is a security allied with death.

Dracul's terror led to no theft of the golden cup, but no more moral society was created thereby, only a more terrorized one.

But the Dracul solution is appealing to many. If offers "the good society" on an easier basis supposedly. In reality, it moves us into another direction, into a non-moral and compulsory compliance with the state.

After generations of civil war, Rome under Augustus Caesar moved into a social order retaining the traditions of the republic while surrendering the reality thereof to an imperial power. Its prosperity could not mask the loss of freedom nor the fact that it was now a slave state. The senate still sat, but it no longer ruled. Rome's "gift" to the world was supposedly the rule of law, but law was now Caesar's "gift" and will. The great virtue became *pietas* or loyalty, loyalty to Rome and the emperor, not to transcendental laws and virtues. The logic of Roman aspirations meant a one-world order, but, with each passing decade, that order meant less and less and had come to be closer to disorder. This is why, finally, the millions of Rome did not feel that the empire was worth defending against a few ten thousands of barbarians. Rome lost its life because its life had lost all meaning. Rome had become mere coercion.

This is the Dracula solution, and it is the death of any society or state. The more a state separates itself from Jesus Christ, the more it denies regeneration in favor of coercion. Its people, learning the lesson too well from state schools, then think of revolution, of revivifying the life of the state by means of death. The Dracula solution then becomes their doctrine of salvation.

The choice is clear: the Dracula solution or Jesus Christ, revolution or regeneration.

Chapter Fifty-Four
Jesus and the Law

The antinomian arguments against the law are strange and ugly. Some letter writers to Chalcedon are so hostile to the law that they actually see it as evil. It is amazing that they do not find their own warped interpretations laughable. Consider the text, Matthew 5:17-20:

> 17. Think not that I am come to destroy the law, or the prophets: I am not come to destroy but to fulfill.
> 18. For verily I say unto you, Till heaven and earth pass, one jot or one tittle shall in no wise pass from the law, till all be fulfilled.
> 19. Whosoever therefore shall break one of these least command-ments, and shall teach men so, he shall be called the least in the kingdom of heaven: but whosoever shall do and teach them, that same shall be called great in the kingdom of heaven.
> 20. For I say unto you, That except your righteousness shall exceed the righteousness of the scribes and Pharisees, ye shall in no case enter into the kingdom of heaven.

First, our Lord clearly tells us that the purpose of His coming is not to destroy the law and the prophets, but to fulfill them, to put them into force. Any other interpretation does violence to the plain meaning of the words. It is eisegesis, not exegesis. *Second*, to the end of time, the law of God, in its very detail, shall stand. Its meaning and intent remain forever valid. *Third*, to teach otherwise makes one either least in the kingdom of heaven (v. 19), or it bars them from it (v. 20). *Fourth*, to teach the law, together with the Lawgiver, Jesus Christ, makes one great in His Kingdom.

Our Lord's high regard for the law, even in its "ceremonial" details, is notable. In Mark 1:40-44, we have an account of the healing of a leper. In v. 44 we read,

> ...See thou say nothing to any man: but go thy way, shew thyself to the priest, and offer for thy cleansing those things which Moses commanded, for a testimony unto them.

Clearly, the day of the priests and the temple was nearly over since the new Temple, Jesus Christ, had come. Soon all the rites of the Temple would be transmitted by Christ's atoning death and resurrection. Their premises would remain, but the forms would change. Yet Jesus Christ *required* obedience to them all the same. Clearly, obedience was very important to have been commanded through Moses. It is now required "for a testimony to them." The word *testimony* is the Greek *marturea*, which means to testify, to give evidence, and it does have reference to a court of law, although used in other ways. Going to a priest who was a public health officer implies here a judicial statement. It is hard to see how anyone can see Jesus as other than a very strict keeper of the law! Jesus thus, *first*, kept the law strictly in this regard, and, *second*, fulfilled a messianic expectation, since it was held that God alone could cure leprosy.

When Jesus first went to Nain, He raised from the dead the only son of a local widow (Luke 7:11-16). The reaction of the people was to glorify God and to say that either the great prophet was arisen among them, or, "That God hath visited his people" (v. 16).

The idea of the modernist scholars that Jesus only gradually developed a messianic consciousness and that He concealed this, is nonsense. It is plain in all the Gospels that He set forth His calling, and many recognized it. But Jesus was not fulfilling the nationalistic expectations, and they waited to see what He would do.

It is held by some that the law was only "an eternal command standing over against the individual who cannot fulfill it," and that "the Law only results in condemnation," and so on and so on.[1] How can this be said in the view of Exodus 20:12, "Honour thy father and thy mother: that thy days may be long upon the land which the LORD thy God giveth thee." Paul calls this the *first* commandment with promise (Eph. 6:2). *First, protos,* means the best among many, the chief. Clearly, Paul sees this as one among many commandments which promises a blessing. It is not stretching Scripture to say that all the law promises blessings for obedience, and Psalm 1 celebrates this fact. The Beatitudes are pronounced on the obedience of faith, and to reduce the law to curses only is to misinterpret it.

Israel rejected the Messiah and was set aside, and the church became the new Israel of God (Gal. 6:16). The law is the expression of God's nature, and it sets fourth His justice. Can we reject God's law without rejecting Him? The church should be trembling with fear at what it has done, but it rivals the ancient Pharisees in its false zeal. St. Peter tells us, in 1 Peter 4:17,

> For the time is come that judgment must begin at the house of God: and if it first began with us, what shall the end be of them that obey not the gospel of God?

The primary reference here may have been to the Temple in Jerusalem, but its meaning plainly includes the church, all who "obey not the gospel of God." A sleeping church needs to awaken. Some Hindus, and also Islam, accept a Christ abstracted from the Bible and His context. Increasingly the church, modernist and evangelical, has an abstracted and meaningless Christ. But the Christ who shall confront them is the living Christ who cannot be separated from the law and the revelation He gave through Moses and the prophets.

[1.] Leonhard Gopplet, *Typos, The Typological Interpretation of the Old Testament in the New* (Grand Rapids, Michigan: Eerdmans, 1982), p. 142.

Chapter Fifty-Five
Power

As we have seen, the number of laws given to us in the Torah is limited, 613 by the rabbinic reckoning, fewer by Christian counts. Again, these laws are mainly enforceable by God, not by man. Those that can be enforced by man are, for the most part, placed in the hands of the family, the specifically religious agency, or the state. They do not empower any institution or agency to control man and life.

The primary solution to problems is not by means of coercion, revolution, or punishment but by means of regeneration. Force is not abolished, because it is needed in a fallen world, but it is limited. A culture that relies on force to maintain itself is already in a process of decay and dissolution. A civilization is constructed on the premises of a religious faith, and it wanes when the faith wanes.

As the faith that constitutes a civilization begins to disappear, what replaces it is original sin, the belief implicit and explicit in Genesis 3:5, every man as his own knower or determiner of good and evil, right and wrong, of law and morality. When men play god, they are unable to regenerate any man. They cannot by their fiat will make of any man a new creation. They must rather rely on compulsion, from compulsory education to strict controls on every man. The state seeks to re-create man by means of coercion.

Thus, the state seeks ever-increasing power, *first*, in order to play god more successfully, and, *second*, it has no other means of changing man other than by the exercise of total power. This means that the non-Christian state, because it exemplifies the presumption of Genesis 3:5, will play god by a continual increase in power.

George Orwell, in the novel *1984*, saw the end of the state's power as the naked exhibition of total power, a boot stamping on a human face forever. The non-Christian state will increase its power as long as it can, because its purpose is the limitation of God, and this it seeks to express by means of raw and naked power. For Aristotle, man is a political animal whose potentialities and power can only be realized in the state. It is held that power expresses itself in order, and order is justice. Christianity, by proclaiming to the Roman world the gospel equally to the powerful and the weak, shattered its dreams of power, order, and justice. These in their true form came from the triune God, not from nature nor the state. The world did not create order; rather, it received it, as it did justice. The laws of God set forth justice, not the emperors, nor the philosophers.

The determination of man and of all human empires, Augustine held, is by the sovereign God and His providence. All power comes from God, and all power rightly used is according to God's law. Man without God seeks to expand his power exponentially, whereas man under God seeks to place his entire being

143

under the law of God. Statist power will increase and develop to the degree that the state and its peoples are not Christian. The non-Christian who wants to limit the power of the state will seek then to increase his own. Humanistic libertarianism is an exceptionally good critic of state power, especially in the economic realm, but it then warps its own position too commonly by replacing the power of the state with the power of the individual to be lawless sexually; homosexual freedom has become basic to all too many libertarians.

The Marquis de Sade pursued the logic of libertarianism, or anarchism, relentlessly. Total freedom for the individual means total power to do anything; every man as his own god means every man as his own law and judge. Karl Marx understood that this anarchism undermined socialism and communism, which presuppose a common order, and hence his bitter attack on Max Stirner for his radical anarchism.

Without God and His law man and the state will expand their powers ceaselessly. Total statism and total anarchy are the outcomes.

The New Testament word *exousia* is translated from the Greek as either *authority* or *power*. The statement of Romans 13:1, "For there is no *power* but of God," can also be rendered, "For there is no *authority* but of God." The word can also be rendered *jurisdiction*. In 1 Corinthians 11:10, *exousia* refers to a woman's head-covering as her authority and power. Very clearly, *power* in the Bible comes from God and has authority in terms in His law-word. When man attempts to exercise power or authority apart from God, he embarks on a path that is self-destructive (Prov. 8:36).

Modern theology and philosophy has reduced God at best to an *idea*. In this it betrays its Hellenic ancestry. It is accordingly antinomian because an idea in the platonic sense is an abstract concept, and so too is law, not the word of the living and omnipotent God.

In Rome, law and government came from the state, not God. Under the emperor Valentinian, codes for the various merchants were imposed on all. The medical care of workers was provided; education was more strictly controlled by the state. Total power was becoming identified with the state.

As against this, Romans 13:1 held that all power and/or authority come from God. What Paul there asserted did not exalt the state but placed it firmly under God. This is a very important aspect of Romans 13:1. A man can disagree with the state on many issues while still holding to the priority of the state. To hold, however, that in *everything* all power and authority can *only* come from God is to undermine the supremacy and independency of the state. Furthermore, if, in all things man and the state are totally limited by God's power and authority, then man and the state have freedom to act only in terms of God's law-word.

The sovereignty of the state means the sovereignty of its power *and law*. The sovereignty of God necessitates the sovereignty of His law and power. One cannot truly affirm the sovereignty of God and deny the sovereignty of His law.

To deny the law is to deny the Lawgiver and to reduce Him to at best an influence, not the ultimate power.

In any system of thought, power and authority will accrue to whatever is ultimate in that system. If it be the state, then the state will be god walking on earth. If it be the God of Scripture, then all power and all authority can belong only to God in any ultimate sense.

Aristotle held that justice is the true principle of order in a society and the only true source of cohesion. He began his *Politics* by declaring the state to be the highest good, and the one "which embraces all the rest." He held that the citizen belongs to the state. Since the state is the highest good, for Aristotle man's hope is in the state.

Given non-Christian premises other than anarchism, the state will only increase its powers because only so can it increase its power to do good. On the other hand, the state under God's law diminishes the powers it possesses and increases human freedom.

What has been said with regard to the state and God's law applies also to the church. Church law has become a jungle of regulations which protect the freedom of the church from God's law and from doctrinal fidelity while giving it license to betray its calling at every turn.

It is necessary to recognize that the departure of civil governments from God's law has led to the criminalizing of the state. The state seeks freedom from responsibility to the degree it seeks freedom from God.

One of the problems of the 20th century has been narco-terrorism. Marxist states in particular entered into the illicit narcotics trade, or controlled it, to finance their terrorist activities. Several responsible writers have documented this development. Other agencies of the state have devised their strategies for independent financing. Properties are seized on drug raids, even if no drugs are found in the house, boat, automobile, or plane. The same is true where environmental rules are suspected of being broken, even if no violations are discovered.

These and other forms of seizures have in common one fact. They provide financing for an agency of state independent of the taxpayer and any legislative body. All over the world, this kind of enterprise is in operation today. A few efforts have been made by some legislators to curtail such activities, but these attempts are dangerous, and the heads of state can easily be overthrown by these increasingly independent and powerful agencies. These agencies have become new praetorian guards who can destroy the heads of state at will.

This development should not surprise us. As the state plays god, it divorces itself more and more from responsibility to the people, to God or to man. Rome, as it became an empire, retained the forms of a republic. It gave the illusion that little had changed when the changes were in reality radical and thorough-going.

The same Constitution ostensibly governs the United States as a century ago, but it is a radically different country and governed less by the president and Congress and more and more by bureaucracies without a fixed tenure.

As a result, bureaucratic fiats are more commonly in force than constitutional law. Laws convey the meaning of moral imperatives. Bureaucratic rules and regulations are experimental supposedly, and therefore unlikely to convey the meaning of eternal truths and laws. With too many people, there is more anger over the warranted death penalty for murder than at the unwarranted seizures by the state of money and property.

Fallen man's dream is to be as god, and so he is tolerant of efforts by the state to pursue that same dream. His hope is in unlimited power as the solution to his problems, and his imagination is given to this dream. God's law has a limited control over man: 613 laws, most not enforceable by the state, should appeal to him, but, in fact, God's law repels him. It limits his aggressive freedom against God and men while increasing his freedom to do good, to prosper, and to live in peace. But this is not the freedom men want: this is a creaturely freedom. Men want rather the freedom to play god. While rarely admitting it, a few will at times say openly that they want an anarchic freedom, a freedom outside the law. How else can we account for the vogue in intellectual circles for the Marquis de Sade?[1]

In the New Testament, one word, the Greek *exousia*, means both power and authority. In English, only one of nine meanings allies the word to legal or official authority and right. The association of the word *power* with electricity enforces the separation of power from morality. At the same time, as morality is seen more and more, not as an eternally true form of thinking and behavior, but as a matter of the personal choice of a life-style suitable to us, power becomes also more and more impersonal and divorced from law. Because the moral foundations, the theological premises, of law have been eroded, power has increasingly replaced law.

---

[1] See "The Vogue of the Marquis de Sade," in Edmund Wilson, *The Bit Between my Teeth* (New York, N.Y.: Farrar, Straus and Giroux: 1965), pp. 158-173.

Chapter Fifty-Six
Law and the Doctrine of God

An important and central aspect of the doctrine of God, rarely if ever discussed, is the fact that the living God of the Bible is the Lawgiver. The implications of this are enormous. *First*, because, as God defines Himself, He is eternal and changes not, the law which expresses His being is likewise the same: it expresses His nature. The gods of paganism are changeable and evolving, but the living God does not change: He is the same, yesterday, today, and forever (Mal. 3:6; Heb. 13:8).

Second, the fact of the law means man's accountability and responsibility. Even some animals are accountable for what they do (Ex. 21:28-32). Whether man likes it or not, the law implies that man has the freedom to sin and also the freedom to obey God. All too many people are unhappy over this freedom. They echo the cry reported by Paul, "Why hast thou made me thus?" (Rom. 9:20) Man sees it as God's fault that he can sin. While man wants the freedom to be his own god (Gen. 3:5), he at the same time refuses to be accountable; he sees himself as responsible to none, neither God nor man. The freedom to sin is the privilege of growth.[1] In the pagan traditions, such as Greek and Roman, the gods sin freely as the privilege of their status, whereas in the Biblical faith God is all holy and all righteous, unchanging in all His being. He is therefore the God of law, unchanging law. Sin is always sin against the Almighty. Man therefore lives in a world of God-ordained and unchanging law.

Third, the fact of God's law gives certainty to life. Right is forever right, and wrong is forever wrong. It is not necessary to wait for election returns to know good from evil, right from wrong.

Fourth, this means that the doctrine of God requires that the doctrine of law and morality manifest the same certainty and unchanging nature that theology manifests. From Ezekiel 22:16 through 25:17, the repeated refrain is, "and they shall know that I am the LORD." God's judgments in terms of His law shall make Him known as the living God, the God who enforces His unchanging law. *The law is a revelation of God, of who He is and what He does and shall do.*

Fifth, to try to by-pass the law in understanding God is to reduce God to the mindless level of the mystery religion deities, a vague, mystical idea or influence. The mystery religions can only be compared to Christianity if we omit God's law from His revelation. Biblical religion gives us, not a mystical faith, but an ethical law that expresses a mandatory way of life.

Sixth, it is, ultimately, atheism to deny God's law because then we are left with a somewhat Barthian idea of God as a deity with an unknown nature as well as a questionable existence. The question is, "Did we make God, or, did God make

---

[1.] See R.J. Rushdoony, "The Freedom to Sin," in *Chalcedon Report*, December, 1996, p. 29.

us?" Because God is the Creator, He is the Law-giver; it is His law that governs us.

Seventh, to deny God His law while insisting on His being is to posit a god who is both good and evil and yet neither; He is merely being without a nature. Such a god is closer to Hindu gods, who equally do good and evil, from the human perspective, because they are beyond good and evil. They have no fixed nature, and their self-expression is unpredictable and terrifying. Such gods are juggernauts who destroy everything in their path. They are beyond good and evil and are terrifying in all their being. Instead of being unchangeable, the gods without law are changeable in all their being, never the same, and never either good or evil. They may one day hate all sin, and, on another, delight in it. They are never mostly just because they deny all unchanging truth and justice. Such a god or gods are madness in both the spiritual and physical spheres because for them no certainty exists anywhere. It is absurd to speak of the law of gravity or the second law of thermodynamics when denying to God an eternal and unchanging nature. A changeable or an evolving god gives us only a universe of instability.

Eighth, to believe in God's eternal decree means to believe that He is eternally the same in His being and His works, and that His eternal self-consistency expresses itself in His laws. God reveals Himself in His laws, and their enscriptured status is a witness to this unchanging nature. Sin is always sin, justice always justice. God's providence is possible because God's being and purposes are unchanging. His providence means His consistency. Sin is a rebellion against God and His unchanging nature and purpose, but God's providence and law work to make everything man may do work together for the fulfillment of God's purpose.

Much more can be said, but it should be apparent now how basic law is to the understanding of God's nature and being. Law is in itself a central aspect of God's self-revelation.

Chapter Fifty-Seven
"A Pandect of Profitable Laws"

It was in the mid-1930s that someone gave me something to read by Hannah Smith (1832-1911). It was a shocking experience. Was this indeed Christianity? Soon thereafter, I read the newly published *God and the Social Process* (1935) by Louis Wallis, far more appealing but still disturbing. It centered, unlike Mrs. Smith, not on spirituality, but on justice, which was wonderful, but justice was rather vaguely defined. In the 1940s and 1950s, I read more works in both areas. Out of respect for Dwight L. Moody, who had a sense of humor, I read many Moody Colportage books, much in the vein of Hannah Whitall Smith.

Recently, in reading *The Bit Between My Teeth, A Literary Chronicle of 1950 - 1965*, (1965) by Edmund Wilson, I encountered this quotation from Hannah Whitall Smith: "When I was young, it was considered indecent to have a baby, and I myself was made to feel as if I was a prostitute."[1] Now Hannah Whitall Smith was not representative of American Christianity, nor its women; she was a Quakeress, of a sect which believes in the inner light, a spark of divinity in every person. Quakers represent a heretical strain, despite their great respectability with the American left. At about the same time that I read Hannah Whitall Smith, I read George Fox's *Journal*, and a life of James Naylor, co-founder of the Quakers. Naylor allowed himself to be hailed like Christ, and Fox, as I recall it, as he approached an English town (Litchfield?), went into a wild "prophetic" frenzy and denounced it as a bloody city for no reason at all.

Meanwhile, I was finding American churches to be either modernist or trivializing. I attended a lecture at one seminary to hear a famous preacher. The girl who invited me saw him as a great light in the church. It was an interesting hour. The man, a noted evangelical, was an able speaker, easily moving people to tears or to laughter, but his lecture was simply pious gush. When I told the girl what I thought of the man, she was horrified, and our relationship went downhill rapidly; she saw my reaction as almost demonic, as she termed the preacher a true saint of God.

I was a lonely bewildered young man. I knew and believed the whole Bible, but, on all sides, I was encountering an alien faith that called itself Christian. There was something dangerous about it, I felt. I learned much later that the writer Logan Pearsall Smith (1865-1946) was the son of Hannah Whitall Smith, which somehow gave me a sense of vindication because I found him so anemic a person, and I saw this as the logical outcome of his mother's faith.

It was not surprising that some scholars saw Christianity in its origins as another mystery religion. Certainly the churches were altering the Biblical faith

---

[1] Edmund Wilson, *The Bit Between My Teeth, A Literary Chronicle of 1950-1965* (New York, N.Y.: Farrar, Straus and Giroux, 1965), p. 115.

to the point that such an equation, however wrong, seemed possible. J. Gresham Machen effectively destroyed that position.

In the 1930s, I learned that a notable Arminian theologian had said of the atonement that its meaning was a mystery. Christ dies to save us from our sins, but how to understand that was beyond man. At the end of the 1930s, I learned from an admiring student of his that he rejected the classic governmental view of the atonement, as set fourth by Anselm and Calvin, because it would give a place to the law which he found untenable.

I realized that, to reject one aspect of God's revelation, ultimately leads to rejecting all. To begin with the atonement means also to begin with the law. Can one believe that Christ died for our sakes, who were condemned by His law, to give us freedom to despise and reject His law? I could not believe that. All the same, I decided to go along with the present view until I felt sufficiently old and mature to write against it.

In August, 1944, I realized how totally at odds my position was with much reigning thought. I preached on Matthew 7:24-27, the two foundations, Christ versus man. All that is founded on Christ endures and triumphs, while all else is washed away and destroyed. I left then for my destination, the Indian Reservation and mission, at Owyhee, Nevada. A letter followed me, from a man in the business world, accusing me of defiling the faith and preaching error by preaching victory. I realized how deep the departure from Biblical Faith had become, and I decided, until I had matured sufficiently to be able to state my case ably and fully, to confine myself to a compliance with accepted opinion. This I tried to do for some years, not too successfully. I seemed to please no one on any side.

I had learned slowly but surely that Biblical Faith is a seamless garment. Moreover, a surrender on any point soon becomes a surrender at all points. It is no pleasure being disliked, resented, and maligned, but it is better than living a lie by far. It is God's responsibility to judge how far these people can go without turning Christianity into an alien religion, not mine, and I am more than content to leave the judgment to Him, but it is my duty to call attention to the discrepancies.

Rachel Ehrenfeld, in *Narco Terrorism*, cited Edward Shils on "'the antinomian temptation,' the reigning credo of America's elite." The "highest ideal of antinomianism is a life of complete self-determination"; tradition, conventions, authorities, rules, and laws are discarded. Self-gratification replaces obedience, and the free self replaces authority.[2] In a variety of spheres of life and thought, antinomianism is today the reigning faith. As against this, theonomy is a powerful witness. Antinomianism replaces God's law with man's will as law, whereas theonomy sees God's law as governing men and nations.

---

[2] Rachel Ehrenfeld, *Narco Terrorism* (New York, N.Y.: Basic Books, 1990), p. 156.

When the King James Version was first published in 1611, its Preface described the Bible as "A Pandect of Profitable Laws, against Rebellious Spirits." None would so describe the Bible today among our many church leaders. Christians then held to the ancient, now reformed faith because they saw it as God's law-word. Antinomianism was then very much a minor view. It is now the reigning position, and we therefore have work to do.

Chapter Fifty-Eight
On Being Holier Than God

It was about the middle of the 1960s that this incident occurred. In a smaller city proud of its churchianity, a young man ran off with a married woman. Now his young wife was a thoroughly Christian woman, highly intelligent, attractive, and gracious. The only "advantage" the other woman had was an appetite for sin. The young man in time broke with his new love, lived with another woman, married still another, divorced her, was involved with sexual orgies, robbed a couple of widows, and a warrant was out for his arrest. Because he had obtained a Mexican divorce, not recognized as valid in his state of original residence, a lawyer counselled his original wife to get a divorce lest he take the house from her; it represented her work and savings. When she did, church after church turned on her and excluded her like the good Pharisees they were. One noted pastor treated her with particular coarseness.

Was this unusual? Hardly. Recently a man told me that his son's wife, a flagrant adulteress, had left him, but he was penalized by the church for getting a divorce.

Now, under certain circumstances, divorce is permitted by God's law, but more and more churches are refusing to recognize this, nor will it do to remind them that God speaks of Himself divorcing His bride, Israel.

There are many facets to this Phariseeism, but one of them is clearly the influence of the myth of evolution. An evolution of Biblical religion is clearly in the minds of many. Dispensationalism is one form of this, and it has arisen together with the Hegelian-Darwinian ideology. Some prominent churchmen have said in my hearing that the Old Testament should be cited only where confirmed in the New. Some have insisted to me that a reliance on the Old Testament is a step backward in the history of progressive revelation.

In 1996, Andrew Sandlin reviewed in the *Chalcedon Report* a little book by the Rev. Jim West, *Drinking with Calvin and Luther*, a good-humored account of the views of some great churchmen on alcoholic beverages and a critique of those who insist that the Bible is against such drinks.

There are many in the church who take a strong stand against all alcoholic beverages. When, in another state at the other end of the country, I preached on John 2:1-11, Jesus turning water into wine at a wedding in Cana of Galilee, I received a very frosty reception.

The reception to Sandlin's review of the West book brought a strong reaction from a handful of people. One critic commented as follows: "Christians need to be held to a higher standard than the Bible."

For many years now, I have heard like comments made with regard to a variety of subjects, especially God's law, which was supposedly given for a backward, primitive people, the Hebrews! The arrogance of such a view is staggering and anti-Christian. Can man be holier than God? And where does man derive his idea of this greater holiness if not from some new god, himself?

In too many ways, churchmen manifest a sanctimonious loyalty to original sin, to their will to be their own god and their own source of law, morality, holiness, and justice (Gen. 3:5). In the Eastern Orthodox churches, theosis, man's deification, is seen as the completion of salvation. The Protestants who insist on a higher holiness, or a higher standard, than the Bible's are setting themselves up as gods over God. Some insist that to hold to the validity of God's law is to take a step backward in the history of holiness and justice. Many who echo this view have never thought of its implications, but some who have do indeed hold to this opinion and are aware of its meaning. Theirs is an arrogance like that of Job's friends, to whom he said, "No doubt but ye are the people, and wisdom shall die with you" (Job 12:2).

What is clear with regard to Satan is that in his three great appearances, in Genesis 3, in Job 2, and in Matthew 4, he clearly regards his morality as superior to God's. He is there to correct God and to rectify God's mistakes. Now we have a like protest: People believe that Christians need a higher standard than the Bible. Amazing how "advanced" churchmen have become that they feel they can correct God and improve on His morality!

Unhappily, there are deep roots to the antinomianism which separates holiness from obedience to God to make it a mystical union with the Holy Spirit. Over the centuries, men have invoked the Spirit to vindicate their disobedience. Somehow, a mystical union with the Spirit places a person beyond simple faithfulness. I have heard of more than one adulterous pastor damn anyone calling attention to his sin as an affront to the Spirit's vessel.

One false argument is that perfect obedience places one beyond the law. But if I steal nothing for thirty years, am I then beyond the law in the thirty-first year? Such thinking goes back over the centuries. One example was the able St. Irenaeus, who wrote:

> 96. Therefore also we have no need of the law as pedagogue. Behold, we speak with the Father and stand face to face with Him, become infants in malice, and made strong in all justice and propriety. For no more shall the law say: *Thou shalt not commit adultery,* to him who has not even conceived the desire of another's wife; or *thou shalt not kill,* to him who has put away from himself all anger and enmity; *thou shalt not covet thy neighbour's field, or his ox, or his ass,* to those who make no account whatever of earthly things, but heap up profit in heaven. Nor *an eye for an eye and a tooth for a tooth,* to him who counts no man his enemy, but all his neighbours, and therefore cannot even put forth his hand to revenge. Nor will it demand tithes of him who has vowed to God all his possessions, and who leaves father and mother and all his kindred, and follows the Word of God. Nor will he be commanded to leave idle one day of rest, who is constantly keeping sabbath, that is, giving homage to God in the temple of God, which is

man's body, and at all times doing the works of justice. For *I desire mercy,* He says, *and not sacrifice, and the knowledge of God more than holocausts.* But *the unjust man that killeth a calf in sacrifice, as if he should immolate a dog, and he that offereth fine flour, like swine's blood.* But *every one that shall call upon the name of the Lord shall be saved; and no other name* of the Lord *has been given under heaven whereby men are saved,* but that of God who is Jesus Christ the Son of God, whom even the devils obey, and the evil spirits, and all rebel powers.[1]

St. Irenaeus assumed, *first,* a perfect sanctification on the part of man which is impossible this side of heaven. *Second,* he assumes further that this perfect sanctification places a man beyond the law, in some higher state of being. Neither view is Biblical. *Third,* Irenaeus insists that the law has been abrogated.[2] While Ireneaus wrote against the Gnostics, in his view of God's law he was in their camp. He held that faith and charity supersede the law, but he did not say how charity was to be defined apart from the law.[3]

Gnosticism exalted the spiritual realm and despised the material, whereas, from the Biblical perspective, both of these spheres are alike fallen, and the answer to man's problem is not spirituality nor materialism but redemption through Christ's atonement. Satan is a purely spiritual being, and this does not make him good. Very spiritual people can be doing the devil's work! Hell is full of devils and men who believe themselves to be holier than God. For that matter, our churches, educational institutions, political bodies, and our streets have their quota of such "holy" people.

[1.] St. Irenaeus, *Proof of the Apostolic Preaching* (New York, N.Y.: Newman Press 1952. Translator, Joseph P. Smith, S.J), p. 106.
[2.] *ibid.,* pp. 14, 181, 123.
[3.] *ibid.,* p. 101.

Chapter Fifty-Nine
Freedom from Man

Tyranny is man's rule without God, and it is obviously very popular because it is so common. Men may complain about it, but they obviously prefer it to its alternatives. Rule without God is preferred by many because they find God's government to be too obtrusive. This is an article of faith with them because, as sinners, God's government makes then fearful of discovery and judgment. More than once I have seen immoral priests and pastors well regarded by their parishioners, who feel then easier in their own sins. They will turn on their church leader only when his exposure embarrasses them.

If freedom were as much loved as men profess to love it, we would see much more of it in history. Men find it convenient to honor things they do not want because the claim to virtue is easier than the practice of it. Pretense is a basic characteristic of fallen man.

What God's law offers is freedom from man. Man's law has always been one expanding claim to power over man. God's law, however, requires virtue, whereas man's law simply calls for moral behavior. In fact, Leviticus 20:7-8 says plainly:

> 7. Sanctify yourselves therefore, and be ye holy: for I am the LORD your God.
> 8. And ye shall keep my statutes, and do them: I am the LORD which sanctify you.

However, for some strange reason too many scholars, theologians, and pastors go, not to the Bible, but to one or another confessional standard when they discuss the law. As a result, they too often say nothing about God's purpose with the law: holiness.

What churchmen fail to see, the ungodly clearly recognize. God's law requires *holiness* whereas man's law requires *conformity*. Throughout history, man's law has at times legislated against adultery, as does God's law, but with a difference. Adultery can be viewed as an offense against the husband or wife, against the state, or against God. God's law is theocentric, not man-centered. It is therefore a matter of *holiness.*

In the Sermon on the Mount, Jesus condemns lusting after another woman as committing adultery with her in one's heart (Matt. 5:27-28). In statist law, adultery may or may not be a legal offense, but certainly lusting in one's heart is not. This is because the Biblical premise of the law is that *sin* is basic to lawlessness, whereas no such idea undergirds statist law. The goal of God's law is that it can be written in our hearts and become our new nature (Jer. 31:33; Ezek. 36:25-29). The goal of God's law is in man's regeneration, whereas statist law aims simply to conformity.

Holiness means a separation and a consecration to God. We are summoned *to become* holy because God *is* holy. This holiness is gained by a separation to God and by an obedience to His law.

In this light, the law has a radically different meaning. The law is God's law, and it must be applied to all spheres of life. Whether in church, state, family, or any other sphere of life, holiness is gained as we separate ourselves to God by His law.

There is freedom under God because we know the limits He Himself has set: His law is unchanging and His law does not encroach on us because its limits are fixed. Man's law, and statist law, have no limits. The next session of any legislative body will increase the number of laws.

The early "legislative" bodies of America were known by such names as the General Court (Massachusetts), or, the House of Burgesses (Virginia). Their purpose was to serve as a check on the royal governor's power and to set limits on the extent of governmental power. Only in time did they become legislative bodies. As they have grown, so too have their monetary appetites. God is content with at best 613 laws. Statist bodies pass more laws in any given session, perhaps. God is content with a tithe, but the state now, in the U.S., takes half a person's income on the average.

It should be clear that our need is for freedom from man and the state. Here is the great slavery of our time, masking itself as liberation. The state that abandons God will also steadily abandon all restraints on its power. Tyranny is then the result.

Men who rule without God and His law are tyrants because they rule without restraints. God's law is a restraint upon man. It also tells us about God's restraining hand, how He allows to man the freedom to sin, the freedom to learn, and the freedom to fail. Men cannot regenerate either themselves or others, and they therefore substitute coercion for rebirth. As a result, the new order they envisage is logically a slave state because they have no power to conform men to their goals in any other way.

Chapter Sixty
"No Other Gods"

In a very important study, Ernest F. Kevan wrote on *The Moral Law*, i.e., God's law. He pointed at once to the departure of the church at times from the truth of God's law:

> ...At various periods in the history of Christian doctrine it has become necessary to reaffirm the truth that the ministry of the Law has been Divinely ordained as a means of grace for the sanctification and godly walk of the believer. This, of course, carries with it no denial that the only sufficient power for sanctification is the indwelling life of Christ in the believer by the Holy Spirit: this is sanctification through faith, and it is one of the great glories of the Christian Gospel that it does not merely tell men to be good but enables them to be so.

> ...What is it that pleases God? The doing of His will. Where is His will to be discerned? In His holy Law. The law, then, is the Christian's rule of life, and the believer finds that he delights in the Law of God after the inward man (Romans vii. 22). The Christian is not lawless (*anomos*) but "under the law to Christ," a phrase from Paul which would be more accurately rendered "in the law (*ennomos*) to Christ" (1 Corinthians ix.21). Sin is lawlessness (*anomia*) and salvation is the bringing of the lawless one into his true relation to God, within the blessedness of His holy Law. The Law of Moses is none other than the Law of Christ.[1]

Kevan held, "All goodness is summed up in the Law, and there is nothing that can be conceived of as good which is not contained within it."[2] The law is given for all men, the godly and the unjust. It was given by God's grace to show men the way to justice. Moreover, "the Law is established by the Gospel" in three ways: *first*, Jesus Christ established the law in respect of its penalties by satisfying God's justice. *Second*, He fulfilled its requirement of perfect obedience. *Third*, the Gospel establishes the law by giving the believer "grace in some measure to fulfill the law (Rom. 3:1-31)."[3] If the law is abrogated for believers now, it must have been abrogated to believers in the Old Testament era.[4]

Now Kevan's perspective was obviously Biblical and held to the validity of God's law. God, being God, has of necessity the law-making power as Creator and Governor over creation. If God is not recognized, then man and the state must seek another source for the law. In the Autumn, 1986 issue of the journal, *Social Philosophy and Policy*, the subject of the symposium is "Philosophy and Law." Most of the contributors are professors of law. As reputable modern scholars, they do not consider God as the source of law. Nature gets a passing

---

1. Ernest F. Kevan: *The Moral Law* (Jenkintown, Pennsylvania: Sovereign Grace Publishers, 1963), p. 1.
2. *ibid.*, p. 9.
3. *ibid.*, p. 82.
4. *ibid.*, p. 85.

nod, but law is essentially a human construct and therefore necessarily a matter for human determination. One of the professors uses as an illustration the moral necessity for obedience of a traffic red light in the desert as against one at a crowded urban intersection. In the desert, with no car in sight, a flat terrain, and no police helicopter, there is no moral reason to stop, or is there? Donald H. Regan's wrestling with this question is not our concern here but rather the purely humanistic approach. We are in the moral world of Raskolnikov in Dostoyevsky's *Crime and Punishment*.

A red light in the desert is a somewhat artificial illustration. Dostoyevsky gives us a more realistic one. Should a person, even if they have not broken the law, be killed because they are socially useless, and even possibly evil? Who determines the right to live, God or man? Framed this way, the moral question applies to abortion. In the early years of abortion, at times the pro-abortion advocates, in anger, would cite the high black birth rate, the low social value of the ghetto black, and like arguments to justify abortion. Their racist frame of mind was obvious, and, of course, the origins of the movement were clearly so.

The basic issue, however, goes beyond that: it is whether or not God permits abortion, or any law that encroaches on His prerogative or violates His law. Clearly, God, as a jealous God, does not regard man's law-making as anything but rebellion and warfare against Him.

Kevan's premise, "All goodness is summed up in the Law, and there is nothing that can be conceived of as good which is not contained within it," is basic. God's law begins with this fundamental premise, "Thou shalt have no other gods before me" (Ex. 20:3), which means also this: "Thou shalt have no other laws before me." Other laws mean other gods, whether we admit it or not. These other laws may be statist or church law, but, unless they are faithful applications of God's law, they are an affront to God.

H. Rondel Rumberg has said, "men who do not bow to God will be bound by man. Also it is better to obey God rather than man."[5] The alternative to the rule of God and His law is always slavery, and slavery is the present direction of too many men and nations.

[5.] H. Rondel Rumberg, *Baptists and the State* (Lynchburg, Virginia: Baptist Society for Biblical Studies, 1984), p. 94.

Chapter Sixty-One
Ultimate Authority

Dr. Henry A. Mess, in defining the term "State," concluded his definition thus: "It is a distinguishing mark of a State that there is no authority external and superior to itself."[1] In ancient pagan states, this was implicitly the case, but since the Enlightenment and the Renaissance before it, religion and morality have been steadily set aside and the state, as its own god and law, has steadily emerged.

The universe of Christendom always had as its ultimate and basic authority the triune God of Scripture. His revealed law-word governed all men and nations, and the final court of justice was the throne of God. The universe was an *open universe* because there was an appeal from history and beyond history against all injustice, and all men had a recourse to that Judge. The statement of Abraham has resounded across the centuries as the confident appeal of Godly men: "Shall not the Judge of all the earth do right?" (Gen. 18:25).

The universe of Darwinism is a universe of chance, and of a random selection which moves upward instead of devolving. It posits endless miracles of chance and holds to an open universe, open to chance, not to mind and purpose. The universe or multiverse of evolutionary thinking is a closed one, closed to God, to morality, and to purpose.

This has meant that this evolving and mindless "nature" is dead to morality. Morality becomes then a human aberration or mores without any basis in any ultimate reality. As a result, moral premises have steadily receded from policies of state. Some morality still remains, but of a humanistic variety. Thus, the humanist holds racism and environmental damage to be wrong. Men like Max Stirner and Friedrich Nietzsche attacked the validity of any and all moral premises, and, in time, these various survivals will disappear. The simple fact is that the premises for all moral judgments have disappeared. Albert Schweitzer wanted to rebuild morality on the basis of reverence for life. After a rainstorm, he would pick up worms on a walkway and restore them to grassy areas, lest they be trampled underfoot. His religious premise was a faulty one: if all life is equally important, then all life is equally unimportant. Schweitzer, in devaluing God and His word, devalued everything, including human life and the worms under the ground.

We see steadily the triumph of the modern state, with "no authority external or superior to itself," in the words of Dr. Mess. This destruction of all higher authority has been destructive to the state's authority also. Crime has increased, and human life has been devalued. More than a few writers (themselves humanists) complain that youths have no conscience, kill mindlessly, have no remorse, and have no idea of a future with consequence.

[1.] Henry A. Mess, *Social Groups in Modern England* (London, England: Thomas Nelson, 1940), p. 118.

The once widely known Christian doctrine of the Last Judgment taught all men that consequences can be eternal, but how many now think ahead? One veteran politician observed in the early 1970s that few voters have a memory of past events beyond 90 days, and no great forward vision. This practical existentialism is a part of the Darwinian world view. In this perspective, there being no unchanging consequences, there is no permanently valid moral law. Man's continuing needs are then seen as prevailing over a changing moral climate.

The statement by Dr. Mess, that "it is the distinguishing mark of a State that there is no authority external and superior to itself," was made in 1940. In 1946, Sir Hartley Shawcross, M. P., and Attorney General of England, said, "Parliament is sovereign; it may make *any* laws. It could ordain that all blue-eyed babies be destroyed at birth."[2] Too little attention was given to either Shawcross' or Mess' words. The state as the new god commanded sufficient faith and trust to render suspicion null and void.

As a result, in and out of the churches, God's law has been disregarded and despised. God has been reduced to a vague spiritual influence, not a Lawgiver. His law is even regarded as evil by many. Man and the state claims final authority. One woman, insisting that much of the Bible was invalid because anti-feminist, insisted in responding to every argument to the contrary with the words, "Well, I think...!" She was the final authority.

The humanistic state will share authority with none, nor will our militant humanists share their god-like claims with any. The result is a conflict society in which more and more people reject obedience or compliance with any law they disagree with. We see a return all around us to the anarchism of the days of the *Judges*: "In those days there was no king in Israel: every man did that which was right in his own eyes" (Judges 21:25). God having been rejected as God and Lawgiver, the result was anarchy.

[2.] Clarence Manion, *The Key to Peace* (Chicago, Illinois: Heritage Foundation, 1951), p. 91.

Chapter Sixty-Two
The Kingdom of God and its Law

Normally, a kingdom has a king, and such a realm has laws. There is no such thing as a kingdom without laws, although, strangely enough, antinomian churchmen do imagine that it can exist. Some evangelicals refuse to call Jesus Christ "Lord," because lordship means both deity and kingship, and, supposedly, Jesus cannot be king until His supposed millennial return.

But "the Kingdom of God involves, in a real sense, the total message of the Bible."[1] In such a realm, "God's law is supreme."[2] The state, however, is not the Kingdom of God.[3] The Kingdom is a much broader concept than church or state: it is the total rule of God in every area of life and thought in terms of His law.

It is a strange fantasy of too many churchmen that there can be a Kingdom of God without either the king or His law. In 1 Samuel 8:7, God declares that Israel's desire for a human king was a rejection of God as King. "They have rejected me, that I should not reign over them." In time, the rejections of this King would be also a rejection of His law.

John Eliot, the American Puritan missionary to the Indians, organized the Christian Indians, during Oliver Cromwell's rule, in villages ruled by God's law. The results were excellent, but to Charles II, on gaining the throne, God's law was anathema. As a consequence, the Eliot book outlining his plan, was burned by the public hangman, and the villages were finished as theonomic entities. Since 1952, the U. S. Supreme Court has dealt similarly with American theonomy.

Israel, in rejecting Samuel and God, chose a man in terms of their humanistic ideas. In 1 Samuel 8, God warns Israel through Samuel of the consequences: higher taxes, the conscription of their youth, the seizure of their assets, and more. The godly form of government by elders or captains over families in tens, of fifties, hundreds, and thousands, would be used to nationalize man-power for the State.

Civil government is a religious entity, and the state, no less than the church, is a religious establishment. Because the state rests on a body of laws, and laws govern in matters of good and evil, every state is an establishment of religion. Which religion is the important question.

A prominent modern aberration is the belief that the purpose of Christ's coming was the salvation of individuals, the saving of souls. The New Testament tells us differently. For example, Mark 1:14 tells us that Jesus came "preaching

---

[1.] John Bright: *The Kingdom of God* (Nashville, Tennessee: Abingdon, (1953) 1978), p. 7.
[2.] *ibid.*, p. 92. Bright is not a theonomist; he simply seeks to expound Scripture.
[3.] *ibid.*, p. 116.

the gospel of the Kingdom of God." It is very true that entrance into the Kingdom of God is by regeneration, by being born again, but the center of the triune God's purpose is not our salvation, but His Kingdom. God's Kingdom is a law sphere, and He provides the law, and He summons His people to obey it.

The law is a covenant, a covenant of grace from God to man. The giving of the law is an act of grace and a blessing, a *gift* from God to His chosen people. Ancient covenants reflect God's covenant. The greater, God the King, blesses the lesser, a chosen people, with the gift of law, whereby the people are to live and prosper. Ancient rulers gave to their vassal lords a law, land, and the assurance of dynasty supported by them. God the King gave to Israel, later to the new Israel of God (Gal. 6:16), the law, the land, and the Davidic dynasty. For Christians, God's new Israel, the land is now the world and their Davidic king is Jesus Christ.

Obedience to God's law, His grace to us, brings on more blessings. "Obedience to the law is not the source of blessing, but it augments a blessing already given."[4] In fact, "Within the Sinaitic and Deuteronomic covenants, law and grace are not antithetic. Law is the gift of the generous, saving God. Through keeping the law man can experience more of God's grace."[5] Because of the covenant framework, "Law is therefore integral to God's saving plan which is worked out through covenants."[6] The humanistic law is not a part of any "saving plan" nor an act of grace towards us. Moreover, the state is not a person, whereas God is.[7] God's law relates me to Him when I am faithful to Him and His law, whereas the state has no personal relationship to me. It is a very serious error on the part of the antinomians to treat God's law as impersonal. Early in the Ten Commandments God declares that He is "a jealous God" (Ex. 20:5). The idea of such a statement in statist law is ludicrous. God's law is His claim for gratitude from a people whom He is blessing by giving His law. Obedience to God's law is gratitude to Him.

As Wenham pointed out, the covenantal nature of the law makes clear that "*salvation is not based on works*" because the covenant was made with and the law given to a people saved from Egypt. The law was a gift of grace. It presupposes grace, and "Law is a means of grace to enter into a closer relationship to their divine king and enjoy more of the blessings inherent within the state of salvation."[8] God declares, in Leviticus 20:7, "Be ye holy: for I am the LORD your God," and He gives His law as the way of holiness. A man who obeys the laws of New York State and the United States *can* be called law-abiding, but this does not make him holy. "The Law itself is the divine means of creating a holy

---

4. Gordon Wenham, "God and Law in the Old Testament," in Bruce Kay and Gordon Wenham, editors, *Law, Morality and the Bible* (Downers Grove, Illinois: Inter Varsity Press, 1978), p. 5. Wenham is not a theonomist.
5. *ibid.*, p. 7.
6. *ibid.*, p. 9.
7. *ibid.*, p. 10.
8. *ibid.*, p. 17.

people. Obedience to it renewed the divine image in man and enables him to fulfill the imperative to 'Be holy, for I am holy' (Lev. 11:44f.; 19:2; 20:7, etc.)..."[9]

Every kingdom has its system of law *unless* it is a satellite state and therefore derives its laws from its overlord. The Kingdom of God is no satellite order; disciplines and realms without exception are subject to it. For churchmen to deny God's law to God's Kingdom is moral insanity and treason. God the King is the overlord to all men and nations, to all arts and sciences, to all things. His law-word must therefore govern all things, for otherwise He is denied and strayed. This present dereliction is an especially radical one. In the arrogance of their sin, these erring churchmen condemn belief in God's law as itself an error!

[9.] Gordon Wenham, "Law and the legal system in the Old Testament," in *ibid.*, p. 27.

Chapter Sixty-Three
The State and Its Morality, 1

One of the key ideas of the modern age is the concept of the primacy of the state. Many came to this conclusion as Enlightenment thinking developed its logical implications. In Hegel, "the state as the embodiment of morality" came into focus and soon commanded the intellectuals.[1] The idea of progress was very popular about the same time, a secularized view of providence. It implied a world at the least backward and imperfect, if not immoral. How then was salvation possible? The church as the saving institution was rather discredited, and the state readily assumed the mantle of the moral force in history. It came to this role easily. The classical world had gained great authority with the Renaissance. The ruins of Greece and especially Rome were especially eloquent to many of the greatness of classical culture. Curiously, at the same time some refused to be impressed by the medieval Christian cathedrals!

Classical culture was idealized. It was seen as a model of balance, proportion, and stability. As a result, the state replaced the church as the saving institution as in one sphere after another the state's authority began to predominate and to govern.

As a result, the state progressively became the answer to the problems of men and society. The state-licensed psychologists and psychiatrists dealt with problems once the province of priests and pastors, and, in the 1980s, there were some who called for the state imposed licensing of all clergymen who counseled parishioners.

The state as the embodiment of morality meant that various departments and agencies of state were created to resolve the problems of men and societies. The confidence that statist answers are the solution led to a common attitude that any opposition to statist controls meant evil and perversity on the part of such persons.

Robespierre had spoken of the good, the pure *people*, but what he meant was *the state*, i.e., the revolutionary state. With time, the Marxists furthered this identification of the state and the people, meaning thereby the pure people and the revolutionary state. Rousseau's doctrine of the general will had prepared the way for this.

Was the church ever the embodiment of morality? At times it definitely tried to be, and still does, but the church is always under the judgment of God the Lord and hence not free to define itself at will. But Hegel's state is the development of a natural kind of immanent deity, its own absolute and so beyond appeal. The state as god walking on earth is thus very dangerous. The

---

[1.] George G. Iggers, "The Dissolution of German Historicism," in Richard Herr and Harold T. Parker, editors, *Ideas in History, Essays presented to Louis Gottschalk by his former students* (Durham, N.C.: Duke University Press, 1965), p. 292.

totalitarian and imperial Roman state disintegrated, despite the attempt to redeem it by accepting Christianity. The result was what Poly and Bournazel termed "the death of the state."[2] From the modern, Enlightenment perspective, such a condition was darkness indeed, and, as a result, the term "Dark Ages" was coined to describe an era unblessed by statism. Meanwhile, the idea of the natural goodness of the state became increasingly popular.

When, in the middle 1930s, Social Security became an aspect of the state's function, there were some who called attention to the inherent economic weakness of the Act, *and* to the fact that the state could alter the act and its provisions at will. Indeed, it soon became evident that Social Security was not a guaranteed insurance policy but rather a statist grant. When objections were raised against the Act, and attention called to its weaknesses, the common reply was that "the government" (as apparently the moral authority) would never permit that to happen.

What is now developing is a growing radical distrust of the state. Instead of being the embodiment (or, incarnation) of morality, more and more people see it as the embodiment of immorality. (This is to overlook man's original sin.) At any rate, man must now seek morality from a source other than the state. The state has demonstrated that it is no more moral than man. Man's problem is that he sees himself as a victim, not as a sinner, and as a result he is morally compromised.

---

2. Jean-Pierre Poly and Eric Bournazel, *The Feudal Transformation, 900-1200* (New York.: Holmes and Meier, 1991), p. 7.

Chapter Sixty-Four
The State and Its Morality, 2

Hegel did not create the idea of the state as the source of morality and moral order. It was the faith of ancient paganism, revived by the medieval monarchs, stressed by the Enlightenment, and then formulated by modern philosophy. Jacob Burckhardt traced the independence of morality from religion back to the Renaissance.[1] Certainly the Catholic monarchs since the Council of Constance saw the church as under them rather than vice versa. The English Church was separate from Rome after Henry VIII, but not unlike the major Catholic states in ruling the church. Queen Elizabeth saw herself as head of the church, and it was unwise to question this. As W. P. M. Kennedy wrote, "She was in a very real sense what Lord North described her, 'Our God on earth.'"[2] Such language was not unusual. Much earlier, the Borgia pope, Alexander VI, was hailed in Rome on his elevation to the papacy with the banner, "Rome was great under Caesar. Now she is even greater. Caesar was a man. Alexander is a God!"[3]

The state as a moral agent, as the ministry of justice in the civil order, is a Biblical doctrine, very clearly set fourth in Romans 13:1ff. What was alien to Christianity was the growing detachment of the state from Christianity and its pagan claim to be itself the source of moral order.

As Richard Weaver made clear, ideas have consequences, and the moral autonomy of the state led steadily to the paganization of society and the rise of the state to the ostensible rank of both god and church.

Previously, the church had been the source of health care, education, and charity. These areas of concern went back to God's law, the law given through Moses to Israel. The early church carried on these duties as God's new Israel. The Christian community had an unavoidable duty under God to meet the many urgent needs of society. The state was a ministry of justice. The church was a ministry of grace. The Christian community had a duty: "we are members one of another" (Eph. 4:25), says Paul, and God requires faithfulness to this by His people, by persons essentially and primarily. Morality is first and last a personal fact and duty.

Because ideas do have consequences, the state as the moral agent has moved into health, education, and welfare, in fact into all spheres of life, as man's hope and savior.

Thus, the state now seeks to educate children and youth about the danger of drugs. As the moral agent, it seeks to enlist family, school, and church in its great

---

[1.] Jacob Burckhardt, *Reflections on History* (Indianapolis, Indiana: Liberty Classics, 1943 reprint), p. 206.
[2.] W. P. M. Kennedy, *Studies in Tudor History* (Port Washington, N.Y. Kennikat Press, reprint of 1916 edition), p. 242.
[3.] Ivan Cloulas, *The Borgias* (New York: Franklin Watts, (1987) 1989), p. 70.

crusade. It complains that parents are not sufficiently interested, and it acts as the primary agent of moral reform. Similarly, "family" education in the schools, state mandated, is sex education on premises which are alien to Christianity but are basic to the state's premise of man's moral autonomy from God.

Adolf Hitler and National Socialism led this movement into *open* moral autonomy from God. Abortion, sexual license, euthanasia, and more were approved, and National Socialism was clearly a homosexual movement. Today only its anti-Jewish actions are condemned as its other practices are adopted.

In the process of this enthronement of the state as the moral agent, the part of the church and the Christian community has been altered. Antinomianism is now well nigh universal, and statist law prevails. The church's role has been dramatically altered. Instead of being the teacher of morality, of the moral order required by God's law, the church has become more the morale builder than the moral teacher. This shift is especially visible during war-time, when the church invokes God's help for often evil causes.

At one time, the church's mission meant a world-wide effort to create God's order. Today, world order is left to all the United Nations, and the church has reduced its scope. In the modernist churches, there are commonly study groups concerned with political-economic agendas derived from humanism. In Arminian and so-called Reformed churches, there are prayer meetings given to small causes, not Christ's world mandate in the Great Commission (Matt. 28:18-20).

The state's moral agenda is dying of cynicism and corruption. Being internally corrupt because of its separation from God, it cannot create a moral order anywhere. As the remnants of its Christianity recede, so too does its shrinking morality.

The church becomes more and more like an ancient mystery religion, trying to give some kind of hope for the after-life while irrelevant steadily to this life. The authority of both church and state is eroding.

F. W. Bussell rightly held that true authority is not coercive. Today law and authority are alike *compulsory* and *coercive* because they are seen as *arbitrary* and even *unjust*. Because both law and authority have a modern meaning, they have become non-moral force. "*Force* has now become the most striking characteristic of the conception of *Law*." Both "State-utility" and the "common good" are inadequate replacements for religious sanctions.[4]

The modern state is morally bankrupt, but so too is the largely antinomian church. The people are well taught in their moral anarchism. Bussell called attention to Pringle-Pattison's *Mind*, with its "libertarian, pelagian, arminian

---

[4.] F. W. Bussell: *Religious Thought and Heresy in the Middle Ages* (London, England: Robert Scott, 1918), p. 648f.

views" and dislike of "regimentation" by God or man. An American writer said of Pringle-Pattison, "God is warned not to tread on the holy ground of the individual unless He first put off his shoes....He betrays a jealousy *of* God rather than *for* God. He is jealous of his individuality, not for human personality as *personalized by God* which is really Hegel's conception."[5] Modern man normally wants only the god he himself imagines as good and none other. His stance is, "Thou shalt have none other gods before me than the god of my imagination." Insistent on his own ultimate, man today is turning on church and state alike when they contradict his moral autonomy. Many in church and state are dedicated to satisfying this warped view of fallen man, and as a result they accelerate the decay.

What must take place is a restoration of morality to the triune God, together with placing church and state, man and society, and all of man's agencies, institutions, arts and science, under God's law and authority. He alone is God.

---

5. *ibid.*, p. 505n.

Chapter Sixty-Five
The Old Religion

What at one time was called in some parts of Europe the "old religion," i.e., ancient paganism, was essentially concerned with magic and sorcery and evil powers.[1] Many would contest Bussell's classification of the desired powers as "evil," but they were certainly not benevolent powers but ones that sought to gain an advantage in society over others. They were *not* moral powers. No pagan sought supernatural powers to be more honest or chaste! If a pagan sought a love potion or a spell to make someone love him, he was seeking, not a harmless, but a coercive power. Paganism, like most of the world's religions, was amoral. The state defined law and morality.

Throughout history, most religions have tended to be non-moral. Magic is more closely related to science because its goal is power and control. The methodology of modern science is sophisticated and learned, but its goals are those of magic, not religion.

With the rise of the humanistic moralistic state, too many churches and theological traditions have abandoned law and morality. Even the great Abraham Kuyper, returning to Calvinistic orthodoxy, did so only by abandoning theonomy because he wanted to concentrate on fighting the influence of the French Revolution without defending the whole of the old orthodoxy. Kuyper's *first* principle was this: "The source of sovereign authority is found in God alone and not in the will of the people nor in human law." *Second*, "ultimate sovereignty belongs to God alone." *Third*, "Even in the realm of politics the Anti-Revolutionary movement confesses the eternal principles of God's word; state authority is bound to the ordinance of God only in the conscience of public officials and not directly so bound, nor through the pronouncements of any church." *Fourth*, there must be impartiality toward organized religion. *Fifth*, Sunday legislation was affirmed, and the use of judicial oaths.[2] Such a statement reads well, but what does it mean? There are churchmen who profess to believe the Bible from cover to cover, but they deny the law, make most of the Bible no longer applicable by their dispensationalism, and have in practice as short a Bible as the modernists do. Kuyper set aside God's law. As a result, he was able to gain only political victories, no true change in the life of the state. He had harmed his own cause more than had his political opponents.

Kuyper had stripped the Bible of its law, and he had thereby left only the state as the source of law. Implicitly, his position was a denial of the possibility of a Christian state. Kuyper affirmed, as against the opposition's insistence on a

---

[1.] F. W. Bussell, *Religious Thought and Heresy in the Middle Ages* (London, England: Robert Scott, 1918), p. 745.

[2.] McKendru R. Langley, *The Practice of Political Spirituality* (Jordan Station, Ontario, Canada: Paideia Press, 1984), pp. 26-28.

neutral state, the politics of antithesis. But how can an antithesis to humanistic and leftist politics be stated without a recourse to the law of God?

The Kuyper years were remarkable because they were a witness to the power and the wishes of a large number of Reformed Christians in the Netherlands. At the same time, they were without a future, because nostalgic and religious fervor cannot take the place of God's law.

Spirituality in a people cannot replace the specific nature of God's law. Some antinomians have been in a continuing prayer circle for some fifty years, and neither their society nor they themselves have changed. One might perhaps say they have wearied God as much as they are persistent but so too did morally dead sacrificers in the days of the prophets. Some of these devout people are clearly sexually and monetarily honest people as no doubt were some of those to whom the prophets spoke. Personal integrity cannot replace the radical responsibility to serve and obey God with all our heart, mind, and being in all things.

The law of God provides us with the morality of His Kingdom. Abraham Kuyper rightly saw the Kingdom of God and Christ the King as central to Christianity, but how can one serve a Kingdom and obey its King without recognizing His law? The idea is absurd, and it invites the judgment of the triune God.

Paganism, the old religion, is reviving all around us, but sadly, it also has a great presence in the church.

Chapter Sixty-Six
Pagan Antinomianism

As we have noted, pagan religions had no moral law. The gods had privileges, and they resented pride on the part of man, but morality meant a restraint on divinity and was for the Greco-Romans alien to it.

But society cannot exist without laws, and, no matter how much man be seen in theory as naturally good, in practice he is restrained by laws on the assumption of at least evil intentions.

The state therefore of necessity had to have laws. Plato's *Republic* prescribed no laws, trusting in the wisdom and goodness of the philosopher-kings. The disciples of Socrates and Plato became the tyrants of Greece, and Plato's ideal order was pederasty, according to Fite.[1] Late in life, Plato did write the *Laws*, but they were hardly more than expedient.

Law came from the state, which was divine, as the case of Rome. In Rome the ruler came to be called *Soter* or Savior. The Greeks had earlier conferred divine rank on Antigonus and Demetrius and called them Saviors also.[2]

Divinity gave rulers like Caligula and others freedom from morality and law because as gods, or potential gods, they were above and beyond the law. This belief is still with us. For example, the world of artists is one of disdain for morality because it is seen as the mark of the common herd.

The Greco-Roman influence on Christianity was deep and wretched. In the eastern or Orthodox Churches, it means platonism, and it leads to the ugly heresy of theosis, salvation as deification, which means that the Satanic temptation of Genesis 3:5 is made the way of salvation. In the West, Aristotle triumphed over Plato, and, with Calvin, the uprooting of the Greek tradition began.

Meanwhile, the Renaissance had revived classical ideas and platonism. This influence was basic to the Enlightenment, and European culture was Hellenized. By the Victorian era, it led to the twelve volume history of *Greece* by George Grote (1846). Law is only incidentally referred to by Grote.

The blind worship of things Greek in 19th century Europe is startling. Richard Jenkyns observed that Homer was seen as the Bible of the Greeks. Amazingly, Gladstone was eager to make it "the Bible of the English too." Other English scholars, writers, and others shared in the worship of things Greek. John Stuart Mill's devotion to Socrates was startling. In reviews by Grote, "he suddenly described Socrates as a sort of savior."[3] This adulation led more than a few to accept or to approve of male homosexuality because the Greeks had

---

1. Warner Fite, *The Platonic Legend* (New York, Charles Scribner's Sons, 1934), pp. 97-112.
2. Edward Fides, "The Beginnings of Caesar Worship," in T. F. Tout and James Tait, editors, *Historical Essays, by Members of the Owens College, Manchester* (London, England: Longmans, Green, 1902), pp. 3, 6.

practiced it. The Victorian "inverts" had the "blend of moral earnestness and self-satisfaction (which) was typical of the age." The public-school world was deeply infected by this influence which is still there. E. E. Bradford tried to vindicate the practice in a poem, writing,

> Our yearning tenderness for boys like these
> Has more in it of Christ than Socrates.[4]

Biblical scholar and bishop B. F. Westcott actually held, "Plato is an unconscious prophet of the Gospel. The Life of Christ is...the Divine reality of which the Myths were an instructive foreshadowing."[5]

The roots of this perspective are centuries deep. It has saturated Western civilization *and the church*. I have heard churchmen argue that Biblical religion is crude and primitive whereas Greek thought was on a high intellectual level. The fact is that for the Greeks *ideas* were ultimate, and, because ideas are abstractions, thinking concerns itself with abstractions. Ultimacy in Biblical Faith resides in the triune and totally personal God. Thinking therefore seeks concreteness and particularity. Biblical thinking is marked by specificity, not abstraction. The incarnation is a logical consequence of the Biblical doctrine of God. The Islamic doctrine of God, while seemingly borrowed from the Bible, is very much the opposite. Islam holds, God neither begets nor is begotten. This lends itself to mysticism, which arrives wherever God is an abstraction. In the church, mysticism has had Hellenic and Islamic roots.

Given this vein of abstraction within Christendom, it is no wonder that antinomianism came into its full flowering with the Victorian era, which had not only its worship of things Greek but a growing interest in things Islamic, as witness Sir Richard Burton.

An antinomian argument commonly heard is that the specificity of Biblical law is crude and morally on a lower plane, whereas "spirituality" is superior. "Spiritual exercises" with many have taken the place of morality, and in "spiritual circles" much immorality is routinely tolerated if it is not public and hence embarrassing.

Thus for many God's law occupies a lower plane while they rise up into heavenly places with their spirituality and pious gush.

The Greco-Roman church fathers found much in the Bible very objectionable because materialistic. St. Gregory of Nyssa spiritualized the law into symbolic nonsense. The influence of Musonius Rufus, a pagan Stoic philosopher, held that marriage should allow for sex *only* to procreate; otherwise, it is "unjust and unlawful when it is mere pleasure-seeking even in marriage." No intercourse when coming home from church, or on Sunday! No remarriage after

---

[3.] Richard Jenkyns, *The Victorious and Ancient Greece* (Cambridge, Massachusetts: Harvard University Press (1980) 1981), pp. 204, 230f.

[4.] *ibid.*, pp. 285, 292.

[5.] *ibid.*, p. 243.

divorce, and so on and so on. Such ideas were common to the spiritually minded pagans. "The sophist of Abdena called sexual intercourse a 'minor epilepsy' and considered it an incurable disease."[6]

Marriage and law have at times both been seen as a catering to the flesh, but then who can live in this world without the flesh? Who more badly or sadly than those who deny both?

Is it a coincidence that the church has seen a rise in immorality in its midst even as it has embraced antinomianism?

In the pre-Christian era, the great high priest was Simon the Just, from the time of Ptolemy I. His favorite maxim was, "The world rests on three things, on the Law, on Divine Service, and on Charity."[7] This was a concrete and practical emphasis, thoroughly Biblical. Antinomianism, with its nebulous "spiritual religion," is neither Biblical nor Christian.

[6.] David G. Huster, *Marriage in the Early Church* (Minneapolis, Minnesota: Fortress Press, 1992), pp. 8. 42f., 44.
[7.] Cited from *Pirke Aboth* 1,2, by Charles F. Pfeiffer: *Between the Testaments* (Grand Rapids, Michigan: Baker Book House, (1959) 1961), p. 72.

Chapter Sixty-Seven
Antinomianism

At one time, antinomianism was regarded as so obvious a heresy that few men openly upheld such a view. Antinomianism denies the validity and applicability of God's law as the way of sanctification. Now antinomianism is regarded by many as evidence of true faith in Jesus Christ! Scholars in recent years, lacking a knowledge of theology, have contributed greatly to the confusion of issues. Perry Miller did much to revive interest in the Puritans, and, in the 1930s, I read him happily and eagerly. In theological matters, Miller was able to confuse me in matters which I had found previously easy to understand! Only after putting Miller aside would the confusion subside.

The New England antinomian controversy centered around Anne Hutchinson, and that incident is still relevant because it so plainly demonstrated the direction of antinomian thinking. Two things are of particular interest in that struggle. *First*, for Anne Hutchinson so high an estate in the Holy Spirit was attainable that obedience to God's law was at best seen as a lower estate and legalism. Spiritual responses were far superior to faithfulness to God's law. To illustrate, as a young man I incurred the wrath of a life-long Presbyterian missionary to China, a man who had graduated from Princeton Seminary and had studied under some of its great men. He was, however, a follower of "spiritual" religion. When the problem of very inadequate giving in a particular church came up, his answer was "prayer" and a stress on "spirituality." I asked, innocently, "Why not a sermon on tithing?", only to be wrathfully denounced to the assembled clergy as a legalist! My feeble and amazed answer was, "But this church is already a very 'spiritual' group, I hear, and their giving is still very low." Somehow, the Holy Spirit was less effective than the plain words of God's law.

Second, the antinomians in Anne Hutchinson's day held that the attestation of the Holy Spirit is to true faith, not to works. This is a denial of our Lord's words, "By their fruits ye shall know them" (Matt. 7:20), i.e., that "faith without works is dead" (James 2:26). The answer of some to this is to cite 2 Corinthians 3:6, "for the letter killeth, but the spirit giveth life." This certainly is amazing, to use Scripture to discount Scripture! In 2 Corinthians 3:6 Paul simply says that the Lord has made him a minister of God's grace in Jesus Christ. The law is a sentence of death to sinners (a necessary sentence), but the grace of God through Jesus Christ is a life-giving gift of the Spirit. If the death sentence of the law on sin is to be done away with by the gift of the Spirit (if we assume that the gift is the Spirit rather than life, a misreading of this text), then we must assume that death is abolished because the law is abolished! Such a conclusion has been reached by a few extreme antinomians, in fact. But Paul's words are far removed from anything antinomian.

In the Reformation era, John Agricola, c. 1538, greatly promoted antinomianism. He denied the necessity of good works, nor could ill works hinder our salvation. During the English Puritan era, the freedom of the day revealed many antinomian groups with radically amoral ideas. They held that sins could not affect their eternal destiny if they had accepted Christ. This was not a doctrine of eternal security but of justification without sanctification.

Some antinomians have held that God's law is binding on the unregenerate but not on the redeemed. Christ is said to have abolished the law in its entirety. Hal Lindsey holds that the law of God "should serve as a 'pattern' for civil law, as John Calvin taught," but not for Christians.[1] What does this mean? Believe in Jesus Christ, and you can break God's law?

John Wesley said that antinomianism is the doctrine which makes void the law through faith, i.e., a kind of exalted Christian Science. The law as a death penalty against us is indeed made void in Christ because He assumes its death penalty, but it is *not* eliminated as God's appointed way of life for us. Agricola was so hostile to the law in any capacity that he held against Luther, "All who follow Moses must go to the Devil; to the gallows with Moses." Like statements are made in our own time.

Antinomianism, by denying God's law, denies His justice. It then has only a vague spirituality and feelings to offer; Christianity is reduced to pious gush; it becomes less effective and increasingly puerile.

[1.] Hal Lindsey, *The Road to Holocaust* (New York, N.Y.: Bantam Books, 1989), p. 197.

Chapter Sixty-Eight
Law and the Last Judgment

Law is the expression of one aspect of God's being and nature, His righteousness or justice. The law is necessary, among other things, for the understanding of God. Without the revelation of His law, we would not know the nature of the Biblical God.

Then too the fact of sin necessitates law. Law helps us to define sin. The Ten Commandments tell us what sin is and therefore what righteousness or justice is.

Even humanists must have law, or something resembling it. They may insist that man is naturally good, but, because he is "anti-social," either because of civilization (after Rousseau), or capitalism (according to Marx) he must be judged and punished. These humanistic substitutes for God's law are far more severe in their penalties than is God's law. The horrors of the French Revolution, with its Reign of Terror, and the Russian Revolution and its Soviet regime, with its many, many millions of victims, witness to this. Marxism replaced law with regulation and psychiatric "evaluations" and terror, but these were only evasions of the idea of law.

Within Christendom, as Harold J. Berman has shown in *Law and Revolution*, law is related to atonement.[1] The penalty for sin is death. Atonement requires as restitution the death penalty, which Christ assumes for us. Men are redeemed from God's death penalty by Christ's death.

In crimes one against the other, men must pay either the death penalty or some kind of monetary or substantial restitution. God's law has as basic to it the fact of restitution.

Humanistic law has self-salvation as its basic ingredient. The prison cell, like the monastic cell, was supposed to be a place of contemplation and separation wherein the criminal, by his meditation and his "inner light," saved himself. It has not been a success.

Meanwhile, religious antinomianism has eroded the idea of law. Eschatology is still a major aspect of evangelical faith, but a strange development has occurred. The second coming of Jesus Christ has been separated from the Last Judgment. At one time, the Last Judgment was prominent in Roman Catholic and Protestant theology. Now is it only the second coming which is stressed. The second coming and the Last Judgment were once inseparable. Christ returned in all His glory as the great Judge over all men and nations. But how can there be a Last Judgment and a final and absolute court if there is no law? Eschatology has now been personalized. The evangelical believer sees it as his escape from death. From a world triumph of justice, it has been reduced to a

---

[1.] See also Jeffrey C. Tuomala, "Christ's Atonement as the Model for Civil Justice," in *American Journal of Jurisprudence*, vol. 38 (1993), pp. 221-255.

personal escape from an evil world. This is an amazing degradation of Biblical Faith, a reprehensible perversion of Christianity.

If there is no law, there is no judgment, no justice. The "prophecy conferences," so common to American evangelicalism, are simply extra-vagant expressions of an antinomian and mystical religion. Men like Hal Lindsey, whose religion is simply antinomian eschatology, pander to this escapism.

Extremists in this antinomianism will argue against the use of or the repetition of the Ten Commandments as evil, and a mark of another dispensation. This is a curious view. If a God-given moral law is good in one "dispensation," why is it not good in all, since God never changes (Mal. 3:6)? The puerile idea of God common to such thinking is staggering. Such man-centered eschatologies are accursed because they turn the moral universe upside down. The same can be said of any theology that does so. Biblical religion is God-centered, not man-centered, and every departure from this is evil. It is not the salvation of man's soul that is basic to Biblical Faith, important though that is, but the Kingdom of God and His righteousness or justice (Matt. 6:33).

To separate the God of Scripture from His law is to separate oneself from God because such a lawless god is not the living God of Biblical revelation. God's revelation through Isaiah still stands: "To the law and to the testimony: if they speak not according to this word, it is because there is no light in them" (Isa. 8:20). *Light* here means morning light, or dawn. "No light in them" means figuratively no knowledge: it signifies no future. To deny God's law can thus mean a denial of a future to oneself. Such people should be in fear of the last judgment: they can be raptured into hell. A man-centered faith is a fearful thing.

Chapter Sixty-Nine
The Law for All the World

One of the strange arguments of antinomians and of other critics of theonomy is that God's law was only intended for the Hebrews, and that, with the Christian era, it is now no longer valid. But God the Creator is Lord over all things, and over all men and nations. All through the Bible, He holds all men and nations accountable to Him in terms of His lordship and law. When Isaiah gives us an account of God's coming judgment on the nations, it is because He is the Lord over and lawgiver to all. The same is true of the Book of Revelation.

But this is not all. We find evidences of God's law in all parts of the world. This does not mean laws against murder and theft, for example. On pragmatic terms, we would expect most if not all societies to have such legislation.

In one ancient Aztec manuscript from before the coming of Cortez, we find that the root for god in the Nauad language, *teo*, is similar to the Latin *deus*.[1] Restitution was the law, but a traveler could satisfy his hunger by taking a few ears of corn from the edge of a field, by the roadside.[2] For married women, the penalty for adultery was death.[3]

In our time, in the jungles of Burma, Don Richardson found Dyaks have their scape-goat, and a ceremony similar to the Biblical scapegoat.[4] The Yali cannibals of central New Guinea have their places of refuge, similar to the Biblical cities of refuge; a similar law existed in pre-Christian Hawaii.[5] Such examples can be multiplied. How or when these laws of God were transmitted to remote cultures, we cannot say, but their presence is very clear. God somehow had His law dispensed to the peoples of all the earth. Certainly we find accounts, very exaggerated and warped, of Genesis chapters 1-11 in all parts of the globe.

We are told, in Matthew 25:32, that "before him," the Son of man, "shall be gathered all nations," and the assumption in what follows is that all nations *know* the Lord's law. They know it, *first*, because, as Romans 1:18-21 tells us, God's wrath is upon them because His law was written in every atom of their being, but they held it down in their unrighteousness or injustice. *Second*, we cannot assume that Jonah was the only prophet to other nations. Jesus spoke of the zeal of the Pharisees to convert foreigners (Matt. 23:15), and Solomon, in dedicating the Temple, prayed that foreign converts would have their prayers especially answered by God (1 Kings 8:41-43). The converts from among the nations were

---

[1.] Kurt Ross: *Codex Mendoza, Aztec Manuscript* (Productions Liber S.A., C.H. Fribourg, 1978), p. 22.

[2.] *ibid.*, p. 116.

[3.] *ibid.*, p. 117.

[4.] Don Richardson, *Eternity in Their Hearts* (Ventura, California: Regal Books, (1981) 1984), pp. 115-16.

[5.] *ibid.*, p. 724f. See Don Richardson, *Lords of the Earth* (Ventura, California: Regal Books, (1977) 1982), pp. 232, 363f.

many; Psalm 87 celebrates the processions of foreigners to Jerusalem and the Temple. In our Lord's time on earth, the Court of Gentiles was evidence of the many foreign believers.

God as the Creator of all things is Lord over all men and nations. The fact that He chose one people, the Hebrews, descendants of Abraham and his household, does not mean a disregard for other nations. Very early, God tells Abram, "in thee shall all families of the earth be blessed" (Gen. 12:3). The word translated as *family* means tribe, family, people, or nation. God has Abraham in mind as the messenger, or teacher of all the families on the face of the earth. To assume that God had only the Hebrews in mind is comparable to saying that because the Rev. John Jones is called to the pastorate of a church he alone will be saved. The focal point in God's calling of Abraham is not simply Abraham nor Israel but the whole world, all men, all nations, tribes, and tongues. As Kenneth L. Gentry, Jr. has noted, "People from all nations are under obligation to God's law today."[6] As Gentry rightly points out, Paul in Romans 1:32 applies the law of God to all peoples without exception.

Those who limit God's law to the Hebrews are as foolish as the ancient Syrians who said, speaking of Israel's God, "The LORD is God of the hills, but he is not God of the valleys" (1 Kings 20:28), and who therefore decided to war against Israel in the valleys. Our sophisticated critics have not yet learned that the God of the Bible is Lord over all things. His law is therefore a universal law. The greatness of the Biblical God is His total relevance, whereas the evil of false belief is that it limits God to "spiritual" concerns. Some years ago, Eugene A. Nida called attention to the fact that, in some parts of the world, being Christian was identified with very practical concerns. Thus, in one area of Liberia, if a man were asked if he were a Christian, and he was not, his answer was, "No, I don't boil water," because boiling water, purifying it, was seen as a symbol of Christianity, i.e., a thoroughly practical matter. In the Cameroun, a man asked if he were a Christian, would answer, "Certainly! Can't I read?"[7] To limit the relevance of Christianity to "spiritual" concerns is to deny the Faith.

[6.] Kenneth L. Gentry, Jr., *God's Law in the Modern World* (Phillipsburg, New Jersey: P & R Publishing Co., 1993), p. 54.
[7.] Eugene A. Nida, *Religion Across Cultures* (New York, N.Y.: Harper and Row, 1968), p. 10.

Chapter Seventy
The Doctrine of Man and the Law

Four views of man have exercised a major impact on Western civilization. How one views man has a part to play on one's view of law.

First and foremost in its influence on the Enlightenment was the view of John Locke, who saw man as a *tabula rasa*, a blank piece of paper with nothing on it to predetermine its nature. Locke's view was revolutionary in its effect on education. The child's future was determined by the educator, and this meant that the good society had to control schooling. This view also gave great influence to the environment in that the creation of the person was a social task in which school and society worked together to mold the child into the desired person. This was the Enlightenment view, and the Enlightenment saw reason and science as determinative in society. Much later, thinkers separated experimentation from rationalism, but, in their beginnings in the Enlightenment, the two were very closely linked.

A *second* view of man came with Jean-Jacques Rousseau, who insisted on the natural goodness of the child and the corrupting nature of civilization. This view was a development of Locke's view, the neutrality of human nature, but it stressed the *innocence* of the child. In the poetry of William Wordsworth, this view, the essence of Romanticism, gained even more development.

In the Lockean view, education became a major concern of the state in due time. Man, it was held, is what his schooling makes him. Wherever Locke's thinking prevailed, so too did public education. The welfare of society and the future of man were held to require it.

In Locke's view, there was an implicit view of the innocence of the child, a clean slate in the world to be preserved and developed in its pure estate. In Rousseau's view, this innocence found expression in the general will as it prevailed in society. Being pure, this general will could be coercive because what it required was for man's good. This meant that democratic totalitarianism became the goal of society.

Third, a curious view developed among disillusioned humanists, and George Orwell expressed it best. The pessimism of his works, notably *1984*, was due to his view of man. The radical depravity of man was affirmed. Behind humanistic man's idealistic slogans about the future of mankind was a grim, "realistic" version of a boot stamping on a human face forever. Whether he liked it or not, Orwell's view of man made the totalitarian state a sad necessity. Total depravity requires total control, but with the controls all in the hands of equally depraved men. Hence the result is a boot stamping on a human face forever, to use Orwell's expression.

Fourth, the Biblical doctrine of man is that he is a sinner in revolt against God. His total depravity means that his societies will always end up as Towers of

185

Babel, dictatorships seeking salvation in a one-world order which compounds all evils.

For Scripture, man in Adam is born into sin and death, but in Jesus Christ, the last Adam, he can become a new creation, born into life and righteousness, or justice.

The solution then is not coercion but conversion, to create then a social order given to justice, to God's law. Man then, instead of making demands of life, turns from the ethos of rights to the ethics of duties, to covenantalism under God. This means a social order in which Biblical law prevails and is possible because man is redeemed man, one who delights to keep God's law. Law then is not an enemy, as it is for the lawless, but the blessed way of life.

On any other premise, Locke, Rousseau, or Orwell, man will be a law-breaker and a rebel. A law society is only possible where sovereign grace rules and men, covenantally, see God's law as His grace to us.

Chapter Seventy-One
Reason and Natural Law

It is well known that Protestant Arminianism is a revival of medieval Roman Catholic scholasticism without its ecclesiology or doctrine of the church. Because of their common presuppositions, all the same there are connections between Roman Catholic and Protestant Arminian views of the church. Augustine was in some ways the father of the Roman Catholic view of the church, and also the Arminian doctrine. Augustine, because of his amillennialism, saw no hope in world redemption. Rather, the church itself was the kingdom of God, called to save souls out of a perishing world, not to make the kingdoms of this world the kingdom of Christ.

Wherever Protestantism has abandoned postmillenialism and its mandate for conquering the world through and for Christ, it has developed a high doctrine of the church. In such thinking, in amillenial circles, the church is the Kingdom, as with Rome. In premillenialism, souls are saved only, not institutions and nations reclaimed for Christ. Arminianism has natural affinities to Rome, and, not surprisingly, some Arminian theologians have become Protestant Thomists.

When any theology, whether Eastern Orthodox, Roman Catholic, or Protestant, drops Scripture as the sole rule and guide of faith and life, it thereby affirms man and his reason as the guide.

St. Thomas Aquinas held, law "is nothing else than an ordinance of reason for the common good."[1] Moreover, "law devotes a kind of plan directing acts toward an end."[2]

Given this premise, Aquinas looked to reason to know the law and to define it. In his discussion of law, natural law thus becomes more important than Biblical law. Aquinas showed more respect for God's law than most of his successors, but he laid the foundation for supplanting God's revealed law with natural law, or, whatever man's reason chooses to call natural law.

The consequences of this are very grave. If law is known by reason's investigation of nature, not by divine revelation, then reason becomes more important than revelation. The revealed law of God is reduced to a measure for the Hebrews essentially, whereas the law of nature is eternal.

Law is the expression of sovereignty. "The sovereign is above the law."[3] Thomas held that "the eternal law is the Divine reason."[4] This eternal law is apprehended by man's reason rather than by revelation. Natural law leads to the priority of reason which in time means that God's revealed law is ad hoc law.,

---

[1.] St. Thomas Aquinas, *Treatise on Law* (Summa Theologica, Questions 90-97. Washington, D.C.: Regnery Gateway, 1987 printing).
[2.] *ibid.*, p. 43.
[3.] *ibid.*, p. 101.
[4.] *ibid.*, p. 45.

i.e., for a particular time and place and without wider application. This, in fact, is the conclusion drawn by antinomians. God's law is limited to the Hebrew commonwealth and is not for us. Some then follow by applying this ad hoc premise to salvation, namely, they hold that Old Testament salvation was by works, or by animal sacrifices, whereas New Testament salvation is by Christ's blood. This kind of dispensationalism led early to Joachim of Flora's three age idea with a different scheme of salvation for each age.

Consistent postmillenialism holds to the same plan of salvation always, and to the unchanging validity of God's law. Those disagreeing with this should logically join with Rome.

Reason as the law-giver has many dangers, apart from being unbiblical and false. To look to reason and the natural law to know God's law for us is hardly sensible. To questions such as, What does the natural law tell us about adultery? What does natural law tell us about parental powers? All one gets is the voice of a proud and arrogant naturalist.

Historically, the abandonment of theonomy, of God's law, has led to the priority of man's reason, to rationalism, and to natural law thinking.

Except within the churches, natural law thinking is virtually dead. The Enlightenment revolted against the priority of God and His law in favor of Nature and natural law. But, with Darwin, Nature became blind, purposeless, and this created a moral crisis. Law was quickly relocated in the state and its "sovereign" will, with grim results.

The churches, in both the medieval era and in the 17th century Protestantism, turned to reason and natural law in revolt against God and His law. They have become the first victims of that intellectual revolution. They continue in their moral blindness to affirm their exploded tenets, and they insist that, unless man's reason be affirmed, there is no reason in the universe! This is arrogance indeed. Rationalism then ends in irrationalism, and its laws become despised and broken.

Chapter Seventy-Two
Sin and Law

In the latter 1950s, when visiting my father, I found some of his old country friends, fellow Armenians from Van Province. Their happy talk turned somber as they turned to the American scene. These were the easy years of Dwight D. Eisenhower's presidency and a relaxed and confident outlook. But these elderly Armenians were full of grief. They saw too well the drift away from Christian moorings into a meaningless and indifferent concern, to an economic republic from a Christian republic. Some shed tears as they concluded that the United States could become another Turkey.

I was shocked by their outlook. Later, when the presidential election, between John F. Kennedy and Richard M. Nixon took place, I was further startled because my father, ill and dying, cast an absentee ballot for Kennedy against Nixon as a protest vote.

As a young man, in my 40s, I said nothing to the older men, but I did not forget that day. Gradually, I came to recognize the validity of their perspective. The Christian past of the United Sates was steadily becoming simply that, its past. No more than Rehoboam could count on David's and Solomon's achievements as his personal credit could 20th century America reckon its past as a present asset.

A great revolutionary pope, Gregory VII, whatever his errors, was radically right in declaring that what must govern us is not custom nor tradition but the truth. He held, "The Lord hath not said, 'I am tradition,' but 'I am the truth.'" The best tradition becomes barren and empty of meaning when separated from the truth. The Biblical emphasis is radically and totally on the truth, not on tradition. We are not ruled by the sons of Moses, nor by the blood line of Peter, but by the truth of God; it is not a matter of descent but of truth. Our forms may be, in church and state, as severely correct as possible, but they are worthless unless the very Spirit of God governs them.

The modern age has been full of nonsense from Descartes on. Ludwig Feuerbach (1804-1872) held that "Being is one with eating....Man is what he eats."[1]

With a background of many such absurd views, the modern era has inevitably drifted from and abandoned its Christian foundations. Having rejected God, it has rejected the doctrine of sin. Sin presupposes God and His law. The sovereign Lawgiver decrees what is good and evil, and what is law, and what is sin. As Kevan observed, "If there is sin, there must also be Law, for sin is the transgression of the law (1 John iii.4)."[2] To deny sin, to deny that moral offenses

---

[1] Cited by Gordon H. Clark, *Thales to Dewey* (Jefferson, Maryland: Trinity Foundation (1957) 1985), p. 475.

are essentially against God and His law, is to deny God's law. *Crime* is essentially against the state and its order; *sin* is against God and His law. Men can escape the eyes of the state, but not of God.

To abandon Christianity is to embrace statism or anarchism, the sovereign state, or the sovereign man. The sovereign God is rejected. The United States, in its drift, has left God's sovereignty for that of the state. It knows no law save that of the state, or some international civil order. The lawgiver becomes the new creator. It was said, of Ezra Pound, "Pound attempted to recreate the whole world in the image of himself and his poetry." In 1922, in Italy, Pound announced, "that the Christian Era was over, and that the 'Pound Era' had begun."[3] This was entirely logical. If we deny Christ, we place ourselves in a godless world and era. But we do not lessen God, nor His law and power, only ourselves.

By abandoning Christianity, the United States and other nations have abandoned law *and* freedom for the anarchy of self-willed men. The Pound Era means anarchy and death.

[2.] Ernest F. Kevan, *The Moral Law* (Jenkinstown, Pennsylvania: Sovereign Grace Publishers, 1963), p. 88.

[3.] Peter Ackroyd, *Ezra Pound* (London, England: Thames and Hudson, 1980), pp. 116, 61.

Chapter Seventy-Three
No Law, No Morality

We can, with the greatest clarity, say, "No God, no morality." Matthew Arnold was foolish enough to believe that God could be dropped from the minds of men but morality retained. In recent years, the validity of Christian morality has been openly challenged. The ethical standard of humanism is against any universally valid morality. The "values clarification" courses taught in many state schools insist on every person's "right" to create their own personal and private morality. Objections to teaching chastity in state school "family" courses are at times openly based on the fact that chastity is an emphasis on Biblical morality. Humanism demands freedom for a variety of sexual expressions.

According to 1 John 3:4, "Whosoever committeth sin transgresseth also the law: for sin is the transgression of the law." Antinomianism, by denying the law denies thereby the reality of sin. Sin is the transgression of the law of God; if there is no law, there is then no sin.

But this is not all. If there is no sin, there is no need for atonement. As evangelicalism has become increasingly antinomian, it has also steadily lost the meaning of Christ's atonement. Instead of atonement satisfying the justice of God by the substitution of the sinless incarnate Son of God as our sin-bearer, atonement has become an emotional event. The evangelical churchmen even refer to the cross as "a great mystery." They can speak emotionally of the shed blood of Jesus without knowing why it was shed, nor why God's law and justice require atonement.

This ignorance has had a shattering affect on the life of faith. The atonement is a juridical act and much, much more. In contemporary evangelical thinking, Christ's death on the cross is limited in its meaning to a purely personal application. That such an application is valid is true *only* if the theological meaning is maintained. If God requires restitution as the basis of man's relationship to Himself, and therefore as necessary for man's relationship in society to his fellow men (Ex. 22), then Christ's atonement is central to the justice system, to man's relationship to God, and to man's relationship to his fellow men.

Without this centrality of the atonement to all of life, to our relationship to God and to man, we have no justice in any Biblical sense. Justice rests on atonement, on restitution, and apart from this religion and society fall into injustice.

Those who insist on antinomianism as the valid meaning of the New Testament do not face up to the requirement of Matthew 5:17-20. Those who "break one of these least commandments, and shall teach men so...shall be called the least in the kingdom of heaven." This does not speak of antinomians but simply of any who set aside the least commandment by their interpretation thereof. Those, however, who nullify the whole of God's law, like the scribes and Pharisees, "shall in no case enter into the kingdom of heaven." It is amazing that some men can read this and insist on some alien meaning. How much worse it is when some have actually taught that the law was given by Satan. Almost all these antinomian "Bible teachers" do stop short of saying that the law's origin was in Satan, but they still treat it as an evil thing too often.

In all this, the antinomians are like the humanists who, denying God, deny His law, a logical step. The churchmen who deny the law have in effect denied God also. They forget that the modernist began by challenging and denying the Pentateuch, the Mosaic books, as authentic. The evangelical camp seems to be on the same pilgrimage to unbelief. It is not surprising that the denial of the Mosaic books is commonly followed by an altered view of Biblical infallibility. More than a few denominations, seminaries, and colleges that began by breaking away from the "mainline" churches are soon involved in antinomianism and loose views of the Bible and its authority. After all, to reject God's law means rejecting much of both the Old and New Testaments. It should not surprise us that many antinomian pastors and churches have serious moral problems whose roots are in their antinomianism. This should be no surprise. If a church objects to the use of the Ten Commandments in its services, it will logically reject their application in their personal lives. If there is no law, there is no morality. Of the ungodly, David says, "there is no fear of God before his eyes" (Ps. 36:1), a verse cited by Paul in Romans 3:18 in an important context, the description of the ungodly (Rom. 3:10-23). It is a mark of evil that this can be said of so many *within* the church.

Chapter Seventy-Four
Theonomy vs. Tyranny

Man's choice is between theonomy and autonomy, God's law versus self-law. Man, being a sinner, a fallen creature, can only create laws and societies which, in their developed form, simply amplify man's sin. The result is tyranny, rule without God.

The power to make laws is the mark of lordship, sovereignty, or explicit or implicit divinity. According to William Pitt, Earl of Chatham, "Unlimited power is apt to corrupt the minds of those who possess it, and this I know, my lords, that where law ends, Tyranny begins." Edmund Burke, a year later, 1771, said, "The greater the power, the more dangerous the abuse." Both men made their comments in response to the John Wilkes affair. Wilkes represented the unfettered will of the people as against a still lingering belief in a higher law.

The word *tyranny* comes from the Latin *tyrannos*; it means normally rule by an oppressive power, but, very commonly, tyrannies have been popular. Thus, Adolf Hitler was clearly a man with a popular following, as was Mussolini, and others as well. A tyranny can be a popularly elected party, or group of men, so that a tyranny can exist without a single tyrant. The essence of the tyranny is that no absolute and God-ordained law and justice prevails, only the will of a man, a group or party of men, or a majority or a minority of men. The essence of tyranny is that it represents in some form the will of man, not the law of God. On the other hand, theonomy means literally *the law of God*. In our time, theonomy represents to all too many people the essence of evil, for the will of man is held to be the source of determination, of law, and morality.

As various areas of society, and its peoples, enthrone autonomy, they dethrone theonomy, and they replace God with man. Thus, in one church after another, to all practical intent God's law has been replaced by man's, and the rules and canons of the church tend to prevail over God's law. In issues relating to sexuality, homosexuality, abortion, and euthanasia, this has been especially the case. Tyranny in the church as in the state is tied to this substitution of man's law for God's law.

Tyranny, rule without God's law, is inescapable where theonomy is set aside. The very statement of the need for theonomy nowadays inflames unbelievers and churchmen alike and the difference between them is often in name only.

The tyrants are earnest men, from the days of the Tower of Babel to the present. They believe that they are alone capable of saving the world by means of their planned world order. Implicit in their stand is the belief that the Bible is wrong, and Jesus Christ was wrong. As an instructor training car salesman in positive thinking as a means of increasing sales holds, Jesus was a negative thinker and a failure.

The Thirty Tyrants of Greece, pupils of Plato, wanted to save Greece, and they helped to destroy it. Much of the world's evil presents itself as the true good, and a failure to recognize the moral earnestness of evil can be deadly. The new pornography does not see itself as the purveyor of dirty books but as the source of true enlightenment, as the basis of the liberation of man. Its fervor often is marked by a missionary zeal.

Tyranny is increasing the world over. The decline of the Soviet Empire made way for other and more extensive tyrannies. The moral warfare underway is more deadly than nuclear war.

Jesus Christ is our Redeemer King, our law-giver from the foundation of the world. The insane interpretations of Matthew 5:17-20 which seek to separate Jesus from the law tell us more about the blindness and/or depravity of such men than they do about the Bible. But all men must be taught. In Isaiah's words, "For precept must be upon precept, precept upon precept; line upon line, line upon line; here a little, and there a little" (Isa. 28:10).

Appendix
The Private and the Public Domain

Some years ago, I spoke at the University of Notre Dame Law School on *The State as an Establishment of Religion,* subsequently published in *Freedom and Education:* Pierce v. Society of Sisters *Reconsidered.*[1] At that conference, I met Edward J. Murphy, at that time dean of the law school. We at once found it eminently easy to converse because we both shared a belief in the necessity for a theological perspective in every area of life and thought. We both believed that theology must always be, as it has been, Queen of the Sciences. Because God is the Creator and Governor over all things, it necessarily follows that all things are of necessity under His ordination and to be understood only in terms of Him.

Thus, despite my thoroughly Calvinistic world and life faith, and Edward Murphy's equally strong Roman Catholic faith, we quickly found that we had much in common. Subsequently, Edward Murphy wrote for the Chalcedon Foundation's Ross House books his study of *In Your Justice,*[2] which is still happily carried by us. He expressed interest in writing a study of theology, and he shared with me several writings, including one on the atonement. I urged him to continue his work by developing the implications of Biblical doctrine for law, but he did not find time to do so. Harold J. Berman, in *Law and Revolution,* had done this brilliantly for the atonement.[3] Anselm's work had led to the application to law of Christ's atonement, namely, that Christ's atoning death, a restitution to God for our sins, required the premise of restitution civilly and religiously. The result was a revolution in law which superbly reshaped Christendom. Only now are we seeing an anti-Christian legal revolution which is undermining that Christian triumph. One can add that it is undermining Justinian's legal work and also that of Theodora, whose Christian premises have governed family law until our time.

The theological premises of all laws are more than a medieval, or a Calvinist, matter: they are basic to the concept of Christendom. More, they are basic to the idea of law. One of the unhappy facts about our present era is its disregard for the past, and its impatience with definitions. The *past* is seen as an era of religious bigotry (we live in a very bigoted time), of religious persecution and murders (although our century has seen the highest percentage of mankind perish from mass murders, death marches, death camps, slavery, starvation, epidemics and political oppression, all without the help of the church),[4] of race hatred and conflict, political hostilities, wars of unprecedented destructive power and

---

[1.] Rousas J. Rushdoony, *The State as an Establishment of Religion,* in Freedom and Education, Pierce v. Society of Sisters Reconsidered 37 (Donald P. Dommers & Michael J. Wahoski eds., 1978).

[2.] Edward J. Murphy, *In Your Justice* (Vallecito, CA: Ross House Books, 1982).

[3.] Harold J. Berman, *Law and Revolution* (1983).

[4.] See Gil Eliot, *Twentieth Century Book of the Dead* (1972).

hatred, and so on. Our age's self-congratulations are not in order, but our humanistic overlords are convinced that, once Christianity was shoved into the closet, the age of peace and innocence was surely dawning. By definition, we are the age of light. One is reminded of St. Paul's comment that, in a time of falsity and deceit, "Satan himself is transformed into an angel of light."[5]

Law has been redefined to mean what the state decrees. The Encyclopaedia Britannica, in its first edition, 1771, began its study of law with a brief definition: "Law may be defined, 'The command of the sovereign power, containing a common rule of life for the subjects.'"[6] For us, the sovereign power is not the state but God. We have forgotten that; for the Puritan mind, in terms of a centuries old tradition, *sovereign* meant Lord or God, and *sovereignty* was an attribute of God alone. On the jubilee of the Constitution in New York City on April 30, 1839, former President John Quincy Adams spoke at length on the meaning of sovereignty by the state as against freedom. The English lawyers held Parliament to be omnipotent because sovereign. As against the omnipotence of Parliament, the colonists appealed to the omnipotence of God.

> The revolution under which they were gasping for life, the war which was carrying desolation into all their dwellings, and mourning into every family, had been kindled by the abuse of power — the power of government. An invincible repugnance to the delegation of power, had thus been generated, by the very course of events which had rendered it necessary; and the more indispensable it became, the more awakened was the jealousy and the more intense was the distrust by which it was to be circumscribed.[7]

Adams, as a Unitarian, was at times fuzzy in his theology, but enough of his Puritan heritage remained with him for him to conclude,

> There is the Declaration of Independence, and there is the Constitution of the United States — let them speak for themselves. The grossly immoral and dishonest doctrine of despotic state sovereignty, the exclusive judge of its own obligations, and responsible to no power on earth or in heaven, for the violation of them, is not there. The Declaration says it is not in me. The Constitution says it is not in me.[8]

A like speech today would not be understood. We have returned to the pagan doctrine of the state as sovereign which contains and comprehends all spheres and areas of life within itself. This doctrine will in time hold the church to be no more than an aspect of the life of the state if it is at all tolerated. We must remember that the word *liturgy* in its origin meant a *public work* because religion was simply a department of state and public morale.

[5] 2 Cor. 11:14.
[6] 2 Encyclopaedia Britannica (1771), p. 882.
[7] John Quincy Adams, *The Jubilee of the Constitution* (April 30, 1839), in *American Patriotism* (Selmin H. Peabody ed., 1880), p. 313-14.
[8] *ibid.*, p. 321.

The pagan state saw religion as a *private* matter, hence the multiplicity of religions recognized and controlled by such a state as Rome. The public arena was the state. The great revolution wrought by Christianity through the medieval church, Calvinism, and the Counter-Reformation, was to insist that the supremely public domain is that of Christianity and the church. The Faith cannot become a private matter without a denial of Christianity, or a reduction of it to one of the ancient mystery religions — another way of destroying the church and the faith.

But a revolution has occurred. We see it most obviously in certain areas, such as sexual morality, now held to be simply a private matter and of no concern to society or to the state. In fact, many object to efforts to further chastity or to condemn homosexuality because it is held that one's decisions here are purely private matters and to insist on a Christian stand is to attempt to force on to the public arena a private concern. The same is true of abortion: Pro-abortion women are often uncomprehending, and they see it as radically wrong to legislate with regard to their bodies. "Our bodies" are held to be a purely private domain, and therefore they are immune to legislation in any just social order.

The erosion of the belief that Christianity, not the state, defines the public domain is so severe that churchmen and church members all too often act on the premise that the state is the true public domain and the sole governor thereof. We no longer have a theology of the state, only political philosophies which are essentially humanistic.

But if the *triune* God is indeed the Creator of heaven and earth and all things therein, then the state is not *our* rule-maker, nor the church's, *nor its own*. The state is a derivative institution, an aspect of God's world and order, not its own determiner. No more than any man or woman can choose to create his or her own sexual values is the state able to determine its own values, laws, and modes of conduct. Of course, we now teach children in our state schools to choose their own values, so the collapse of religion and ethics into the private domain is far gone.

But God alone is the true law-giver because He alone is sovereign. The temptation in Genesis 3:5 has been rightly called man's original sin: his desire to be his own god, determining, or knowing for himself, what constitutes good and evil, law and morality. Our culture today wallows in original sin. Instead of the Biblical "thus saith the Lord," people say, "Well, *I* think," or "*I* feel," or, "*I* don't care what the Bible or the church say, *I* think...." We have every man functioning as his own god and law. If a man tells you that he is a *good* Catholic, or a *good* Protestant, it is likely that he has in too many cases redefined the *good* church to suit himself.

Now to insist that Christianity defines the public domain in terms of the Trinity and Scripture means that man is under *authority*. It is important to examine that word as it is used in The New Testament. *Dynamis* in Greek is translated as authority, also as power, capability, force, ability, and so on. Otto Betz said, "Originally it meant the seat of government, and then, equally, someone who was in such a position of authority or strength."[9] The Gospel is the power of God unto salvation, and the cross and resurrection supremely manifest the power of God.

Another word for authority (also for right and power) is *exousia* in Greek. It refers to the exercise of authority by a ruler, father, or some delegated person. Both *dynamis* and *exousia* are "related to the work of Christ, the consequent new ordering of cosmic power-structures and the empowering of believers."[10] The implication is that all non-Christian authority is ultimately illegitimate. This does not mean that we have the freedom to be lawless in relation to them. St. Paul, for example, counsels believers who are slaves to avoid insurrection. Having "been bought with a price, be not ye the slaves of men."[11] However, "if thou mayest be made free, use it rather."[12] Freedom is to be desired, but it is not the only moral concern.

But the insistence throughout history on some sole moral concern has led to serious social disruptions. The Throne of authority is not man's conscience but the sovereign and triune God. It has been Christianity which has most insisted on the necessity for a clean conscience before God. The whole concept of confession, in its Roman Catholic and Protestant histories, has been a history of the examination and the cleansing of the conscience. This is a radically different concept from that of humanistic individualism which absolves the conscience of accountability to God or to man. Since World War II especially, conscience in the Western world has claimed absolution from all accountability to God. This has been possible because God and Christianity are now part of the private domain. This is a tacit assumption that God does not exist and that He is at best a conjectural idea and of no concern to the functioning of the public domain. The relegation of God to the private domain is seen by some as a charitable and tolerant act because God is an idea whose influence is not for the best welfare of society.

Because the state is now the heart and soul of the public domain, it has replaced God, the church, and Christianity in the minds of men. It is the state now in whom we live, and move, and have our being. It is the state which, with its planning and controls, has so replaced God's predestination that most men wince at the thought of God's plan of predestination, but live more or less comfortably with the state's plan. After all, the public domain requires governance and power, whereas the private domain to which God and

---

[9.] Otto Betz, *Might, Authority, Throne*, in 2 The New International Dictionary of New Testament Theology (Colin Brown ed. 1976), p. 609.

[10.] Otto Betz, *Exousia*, in 2 The New International Dictionary of the New Testament Theology, *supra* note 9, p. 609.

[11.] 1 Cor. 7:23.

[12.] 1 Cor. 7:21.

Christianity have been reduced must remain as ideas only — and be grateful for that.

Since Hegel at least, the state has been god walking on earth, the ultimate power and mind in being. This is an old battle which the church has repeatedly fought, lost, and won. For example, the Council of Constance ended the Great Schism by imperial power. The three rival popes were reduced to one, but the price was losing control of the church to the emperor and some monarchs, notably the French, and later, the Spanish. The church was pressured to avoid offense and so turned its attention to the arts, leading to the Renaissance, and then, by reaction, to the Reformation and the Counter-Reformation, which, until circa 1660, sought to again make the church the heart of the public domain. The Enlightenment, with its priority of Reason, saw the state as the epitome of the rational order and the legitimate heir of the public domain. With the Enlightenment, the church, as the private domain, was seen as the anti-Reason realm. Men less and less concerned themselves with the Faith, and they saw the church as the domain of unreason and emotionalism and hence primarily for women and children. Since then, the church has become more and more outside the concerns of men. Now, with the rise of feminism, women seek to take over the leadership of the church as "rightfully" theirs.

In the 1960s, a rising protest targeted moral judgments by Christians premised on any moral character or standard. Morality was a matter for the private domain and a purely personal concern. To object to abortion, homosexuality, or euthanasia, or to insist that chastity should be promoted or at least mentioned in sex education courses of study, was held to be an unwarranted confusion of church and state.

The nature of the rationale behind this has been apparent in numerous works. Alisdair Palmer, in a review of one such book in the English *Spectator,* observed,

> For the last 2,000 years, the central assumption of Western philosophical thought has been that the path of wisdom leads to righteousness. Almost all moral philosophy has been dedicated to trying to prove that no one who is fully rational can fail to be good, because truth, goodness and Rationality are one.[13]

Previously, challenges to this assumption came from men who could be dismissed as mad, such as the Marquis de Sade, Friedrich Nietzsche, and the like. Now such ideas are promoted routinely by academicians, members of the media, artists, and routine citizens of commonplace backgrounds. Palmer cites the fact that Nietzsche held that "power-worship" must replace morality, and Bernard Williams denies that power must of necessity do so. Palmer is not so sure. What neither Palmer nor Williams fail to consider is why morality should, like religion, be excluded from the public domain. After all, how people behave very much

---

[13.] Alisdair Palmer, *The Return of the Antichrist,* The Spectator, Sept. 30., 1995 (reviewing Bernard Williams, *Making Sense of Humanity,* 1995), p. 45.

affects the public realm, and the consequences of a Hitler or a Stalin commanding that sphere are very different from the results of King Alfred's rule.

The citation of King Alfred, now a somewhat forgotten figure, is deliberate. King Alfred was concerned with two causes. First, he sought to free his realm from the depredations of Danish invaders. Second, to strengthen his realm, he insisted that God's law, as given in the Bible, govern his realm. Dominion or rule was for him a religious fact, and it necessarily meant that the premises of a particular faith prevail.

Religion is the "ultimate concern," as Paul Tillich held, and the U. S. Supreme Court has used his definition. The man-ward aspect of religion is morality and law, the application of the nature of ultimate Being to life in all its spheres. In terms of this, men have rightly held that all systems of law are establishments of religion. The current insistence on "the separation of church and state" is really the effort to disestablish Christianity as the religion behind our concepts of law and government and to replace it with a statist humanism. The new, established and catholic church is the state. The religious institution in any society is salvific: i.e., it has either the intent or the power to redeem. This the modern state sees itself as called to do, to save men and society from all their ills. The church is less and less seen as the necessary instrument for man's salvation, whereas the state sees itself, and is seen by many people, as man's hope. It offers man cradle to grave care, or, as the English state it, from womb to tomb.

Clearly, in this long process of re-paganization whereby religion, Christianity in particular, has been relegated to the private and therefore nonessential sphere, law has been separated from Christianity and assigned to the state by common opinion.

Christianity has thus been limited to mainly pietistic exercises, personal devotion and private faith. Because it is a private matter, loyalty to the church, its creeds and confessions, its hierarchy and its worship, is now seen by many as *a private option*. Too many Roman Catholic, Eastern Orthodox, and Protestant believers have major differences with their churches' stands and yet will maintain that they are faithful members by their own definition.

The two key areas which manifest the religion of a culture are *education* and *law*. If these are not governed by the *faith* of the people, then the professions of faith, Orthodox, Catholic, or Protestant, are nominal and the actual functioning faith is something else, at present, humanism. In the sphere of education, Catholic and mainline Protestant parochial schools have retreated significantly. However, a major explosion of Christian schools and home schooling has taken place.

In the sphere of law, a few starts have been made to think through and provide a philosophy of the idea of law. The major effort in this area, by a professor of law in the Netherlands, was the work of the late Herman

Dooyeweerd, most notably in his *De Wijsbegeerte der Wetsidee,* translated into English as *A New Critique of Theoretical Thought*[14] in four volumes. In the main, positivism, as first set forth by Auguste Comte, has been hostile to the idea of law. Marxist theory has gone beyond the idea of law to affirm an ever-changing will of the people via the dictatorship of the proletariat. The basic question of those concerned with this area of thought is whether or not the starting point should be a philosophy of law, or a theology of law. My approach is theological.

There is another aspect to this question. If we see the source of law as the triune God and His enscriptured word, we logically identify law with the being of God. God's law expresses His nature, and the all-perfect nature of God makes it inevitable that His law is unchanging, and it never contradicts His being. Statist law has no such consistency; its changing and variable nature witnesses to the changing and unstable nature of the state. It was Henry VIII who told the Irish, "of our absolute power we be above the law."[15] Because Henry VIII was a changing and very fallible man, his law was equally fallible and unstable. His law expressed his nature, even as contemporary statist laws express too often the fallen and sinful views of men. About 1970, a lawyer remarked to me that law was being replaced by the will of judges; he added that he never knew what the law would be when he walked into a court. In 1974, Paul Hoffman wrote a study of a criminal lawyer and gave that man's comment prominence as the book's title: *What the Hell is Justice?*[16] The law is too often regarded with cynicism in our time because it lacks any Christian foundation.

Some years ago, J. M. Spier observed that "[t] he Christian philosopher must start with the revealed truth that the Sovereign Creator has placed his entire creation under law. The term *cosmic law order* expresses the fact that everything created is subject to the laws of God."[17] God's laws are, like God, unchangeable. Man, because he is a creature, is under law, his Maker's law. Spier further relates that "[n]ot to be under law would be to be as God. Recall the lying words of the serpent in paradise: 'Do not be troubled by God's law, elevate yourself above it, and you will be as God.' But to be like God is unattainable to a creature."[18]

If man is *under God,* then his every area of life and thought will be under God. If man is the product of biological and social evolution, as Henry Jones Ford, then a professor of politics at Princeton in 1915, maintained, it logically follows that "[t]he State is the permanent and universal frame of human existence."[19] Moreover, "Man did not make the State; the State made Man. Man is born a political being. His Nature was formed by government, requires government and seeks government."[20] Again, Ford held that "[t]he State is absolute and

---

[14.] Herman Dooyeweerd, *A New Critique of Theoretical Thought* (David H. Freeman & William S. Young trans., 1969). In some of my works, I have also dealt with the idea of law.

[15.] Lawrence Stone, *The Causes of the English Revolution 1529-1642* (1972), p. 58.

[16.] Paul Hoffman, *What the Hell is Justice?* (1974).

[17.] J. M Spier, *An Introduction to Christian Philosophy* (David H. Freeman trans., 1954), p. 35.

[18.] *ibid.,* p. 41.

[19.] Henry Jones Ford, *The Natural History of the State* (1915), p. 174.

unconditioned in its relation to its unit life."[21] For Ford, the state had replaced
God as man's maker. Such thinking as Ford represented was prevalent and
powerful in the United States for a generation and more prior to World War I.
Given this background, it is not surprising that in a few decades Robert C.
Harvey could write that "grouphood" was replacing "personhood," and that
"[w]e are becoming a culture of un-persons."[22] It is no wonder that, in the
1960s, when rebellious youth sought their "identity," they did so in a radically
conformist way, with a uniformity of hair and dress styles that depersonalized
them. By denying their faith-heritage, they denied their personhood. We must
remember that, in the medieval era, one Northern European people declared,
"We are men and must have laws."[23] Personhood has a religious foundation in
the triune Persons of the Godhead. By trying to ban God and Christianity, the
church and morality and God's law, from the public domain, the twentieth
century has dehumanized man and it has replaced society with the state.

The Bible and the historic creeds of Christendom have an essential bearing on
law. They witness to the fact of an unchanging order as basic to law and society.

We have forgotten that in colonial and early American history such bodies as
the Massachusetts General Court and the Virginia House of Burgesses were not
legislative bodies but citizens' assemblies to protect and ensure sound and lawful
administration. They did not make laws so much as to protect law. It would not
have occurred to them that Christianity should occupy the private domain and
quietly surrender the world to the state. For them, the state had as much a duty
to be Christian as did the church, and, for that matter, the family, the school, the
arts and sciences, and all things else. This was the ancient stand of Christendom.
A return to this perspective is a necessary step towards the establishment of a
viable order.

---

[20]. *ibid.*, p. 175.
[21]. *ibid.*, p. 175-176.
[22]. Robert C. Harvey, *The Restless Heart, Breaking the Cycle of Social Identity* (1973), p. 13.
[23]. *ibid.*

Scripture Index

Index

The Author

Rousas John Rushdoony (1916-2001) was a well-known American scholar, writer, and author of over thirty books. He held B.A. and M.A. degrees from the University of California and received his theological training at the Pacific School of Religion. An ordained minister, he worked as a missionary among Paiute and Shoshone Indians as well as a pastor to two California churches. He founded the Chalcedon Foundation, an educational organization devoted to research, publishing, and cogent communication of a distinctively Christian scholarship to the world-at-large. His writing in the *Chalcedon Report* and his numerous books spawned a generation of believers active in reconstructing the world to the glory of Jesus Christ. Until his death, he resided in Vallecito, California, where he engaged in research, lecturing, and assisting others in developing programs to put the Christian Faith into action.

The Ministry of Chalcedon

CHALCEDON (kal-see-don) is a Christian educational organization devoted exclusively to research, publishing, and cogent communication of a distinctively Christian scholarship to the world at large. It makes available a variety of services and programs, all geared to the needs of interested ministers, scholars, and laymen who understand the propositions that Jesus Christ speaks to the mind as well as the heart, and that His claims extend beyond the narrow confines of the various institutional churches. We exist in order to support the efforts of all orthodox denominations and churches. Chalcedon derives its name from the great ecclesiastical Council of Chalcedon (AD 451), which produced the crucial Christological definition: "Therefore, following the holy Fathers, we all with one accord teach men to acknowledge one and the same Son, our Lord Jesus Christ, at once complete in Godhead and complete in manhood, truly God and truly man...." This formula directly challenges every false claim of divinity by any human institution: state, church, cult, school, or human assembly. Christ alone is both God and man, the unique link between heaven and earth. All human power is therefore derivative: Christ alone can announce that, "All power is given unto me in heaven and in earth" (Matthew 28:18). Historically, the Chalcedonian creed is therefore the foundation of Western liberty, for it sets limits on all authoritarian human institutions by acknowledging the validity of the claims of the One who is the source of true human freedom (Galatians 5:1).

The Chalcedon Foundation publishes books under its own name and that of Ross House Books. It produces a magazine, *Faith for All of Life*, and a newsletter, The *Chalcedon Report*, both bimonthly. All gifts to Chalcedon are tax deductible. For complimentary trial subscriptions, or information on other book titles, please contact:

Chalcedon
Box 158
Vallecito, CA 95251 USA
(209) 736-4365
www.chalcedon.edu